Tad's Happy Funtime
A Collection of Misremembered Events

By Tad Callin

To Kate

Table of Contents

Introduction

The Internet was still a New Thing for most people in 1998. Sure, there had been message boards and AOL for several years by then, and Usenet was a thriving thing full of a bewildering wash of brilliance and filth, but my first real exposure to online culture was through the official military network we used in the Air Force. As my friends from the language school arrived at our various duty stations around the world, we found ourselves connected by this network, and as you might imagine, we did the same thing that every Internet n00b from time immemorial has done: we forwarded jokes, memes, and the 1998 equivalent of stupid cat videos to each other at every opportunity.

I was as bad as anyone in the first few months, laughing like a hyena at the "Student Bloopers of World History," the lists of dubious quotes, or the lip-quivering stories about mothers who lifted cars off their babies in moments of desperation. But the repetitive nature of the material and the formatting errors from forwarding through different mail clients quickly became annoying. Since I didn't have much else to do besides sit tied to my workstation for 12-hour stretches, I became less of a compulsive forwarder of such things, and more of a curator.

By the end of my three-year tour, I had accrued a tremendous collection of Dave Barry columns, lists of piquant quotations, Top Ten lists, jokes, excerpts of Bill Bryson books, and other folderol; but I had also begun writing out my own stories. I settled into a regular rhythm in which I collected a week's worth of email and edited it into a sort of newsletter. I also began to compose stories: some about life at my base, some about the people I knew from the language school, some about my life as a kid growing up in rural Arizona. These weekly newsletters full of jokes, framed by my stories, needed a title that seemed silly but catchy, so I began calling them *Tad's Happy Funtime.*

In 2003, after I had long since left the military, a friend from the language school convinced me to take up blogging. I started posting regularly on my Myspace blog in 2005, but eventually in 2007, I relocated to Blogger. I kept my blog's title, of course, and even managed to reproduce some of my more popular pieces from the early days—like "Six Little Words"—and for several years, these posts accumulated.

People have asked me about my writing over the years, and many have encouraged me to put together a book, but I never really considered publishing my blog posts until I mentioned to my friend Joanna that if I could find an editor willing to hash through all of my old material, it might make a nice volume someday. She did something few people do: she took me seriously.

That was almost a year ago, and this book is the result.

There is a lot that is not included here. I had to leave out some stories about people and events that were (and are) very important to me, and I combined details of some stories to make the narrative less confusing. That means some of my friends and family will see pieces of themselves in some of the characters here, and will notice some mistakes. There are also some stories I thought of after this book was already done, and I had to make a hard choice to save them for later. I hope that you will see the final product for what it is: a lifetime of tall tales told sitting at card tables, on couches, around campfires, and at desks via our interconnected computer screens, in the watches of the night.

Humor, especially at my own expense, has always been the first tool I use to deal with life. No matter how dark or how bleak things seem, humor has been the pressure valve. Sometimes it's the key to survival. As a result, a lot of these stories are funny, but they aren't all jokes. There are some stories in here that aren't funny at all, and some that put a bright happy face on some seriously messed up events. If you think things are getting too real, just remember that we're here, and that we survived; and consider paying closer attention to the jokers in your own life, just to make sure they're alright.

But, friends, that way lies maturity, and I've always maintained that maturing is just a step on the slippery road to senility and death. So please, enjoy some embarrassing and awkward stories, some misadventures, and maybe the occasional poop joke—just to stay young.

It's only life, after all.

Tad Callin
Parkville, Maryland
March 24, 2016

Part I:
Youth

This One Might Be Different

1
Fall

I was up in the air, looking down, and my world tilted back and forth.

I saw my dad, frowning, off to one side, as the rest of the men in the family gathered around, laughing and stacking the metal trash cans inside of each other... while my cousin and I sat inside the topmost can.

We hooted and shrieked with screams of delight as we waved around more and more drastically, the creak and scrunk of the cans growing louder as the men lifted the cans from below and fit them into the next. We rose higher and the stack grew taller.

Dad was a firefighter and had already begun to worry more about physical damage; so the ringleader of the can-stackers was Uncle Dick. Dad's Uncle Dick had been in The War; he'd had two fingers shot off by a "Jap sniper." Uncle Dick was a Maricopa County superior court justice. A man of respect and dignity, and well-respected in the community.

And Uncle Dick said there was no harm in boys' rough-housing.

So my cousin and I sat in a trash can and let the grown-ups lift us higher and higher. After all, the adults were saying, *What harm is there in it? Ted's a firefighter, isn't he? They'll be safe!*

And at some point, the tilting and wavering became the fall. Slowly—at least in my memory—we eased to the ground, which seemed to stay distant until the very last second, when it rushed up all at once and slammed the sides of the cans.

We tumbled, laughing, in hysterics from fear and thrill, into a meager stack of leaves. I don't think it hurt... but that's probably because I was Superman.

At five, who isn't?

2
Prissy and Prudence

When I was born, my parents were expecting a daughter and they had a name picked out: Priscilla Jane. Thankfully, my anatomy and their adherence to cultural convention saved me from that fate. By the time my sister came along, Mom and Dad had planned ahead with *two* names (just in case), and this time Priscilla didn't make the cut. Later on, sometime in the 1980s, Mom finally got to use the name on someone who couldn't complain about it when we had the opportunity to adopt a little black toy poodle.

Prissy joined our household despite the disgust and disdain of our other four-legged resident, a tortoiseshell cat named Prudence. Prudence had dealt with a canine cohabitant before, but Prissy was nothing like our old dog, Maverick. Where Maverick had been an affable and good-natured mutt who had welcomed the little kitten into the family several years before (probably establishing a bit of that Alpha dog mystique), Prissy was an aptly named intruder on territory that Prudence had come to consider her own.

It didn't help that my sister and I treated Prissy like a celebrity. Competing for her affections, we each tried to coax her to sleep in our respective rooms and fought over the honor of "taking care of" the dog. Now that I'm older, I realize that Prissy probably didn't appreciate the stable that my horse-crazy sister built for her out of Lincoln Logs, and I'm sure she had similar misgivings about my attempts to turn her into the Rancor in my homemade cardboard reproduction of Jabba the Hutt's palace.

I suppose it's a credit to Prissy that she didn't let all of the attention go to her head. Maybe not, since there wasn't much in her head to begin with. She put up with our attempts to relate to her, but she mainly wandered the house doing her own thing. Prudence, being a cat, was at first rather aloof about the whole dog thing. After some sparks struck during their first few meetings, she elected to pretend that there was no dog in her house, and for a while they got along splendidly by not interacting.

This began to change when Mom decided to try breeding Prissy. We didn't have papers proving anything, but Prissy was supposed to be a pure toy poodle, and one of mom's friends had a boy toy (poodle) named Pepper—so they decided to try their hand at animal husbandry. We borrowed Pepper for a week or so when mom predicted Prissy would be in heat—and despite the fact that Pepper was a lot younger and smaller than Prissy, apparently magic happened.

Looking back, this was probably where I learned about sexual reproduction, but being both Southern Baptist and born with our family's sense of humor, I don't think I learned about it in as direct and matter-of-fact a manner as I might have under other circumstances. I would hear the adults plotting out Prissy's cycle, and I remember asking what "in heat" meant; I think they told me that was the time in a month when Prissy could have puppies. Since the week came and went with no puppies, I didn't really get the connection until much later.

The connection I did make was with Prissy's array of "gentleman callers"—all of the male dogs in our remote stretch of barely-settled desert could smell her, and they came parading by our house at all hours. Terriers, shepherds, setters, and a few dodgy-looking characters who might not have been entirely domesticated found their way through our fence and onto our porch, where they curled up and waited for a glimpse of the source of the alluring scent that was pulling them to our door.

For several years, there was an uneasy monthly ritual that surrounded leaving our house. We had to check the door before opening it to leave, and if it was too crowded on the porch, we would sneak out the side or back door. Dad tried patching places in the fence where the dogs got in, but there were always a few eager diggers around the neighborhood. Even when the fence held, they just gathered at the gate, waiting to dart in when we tried to get our car out.

The most patient and brazen of these horny intruders was a basset hound my mom nicknamed Frederick B. Moose. He was implacable. He would plant himself stolidly to one side of the road and wait for Dad or Mom to go chasing his bolder rivals off. Then he grunted into motion and trundled his way towards our door. Once inside the fence, he was impossible to dislodge. Mom and Dad each tried to drag him out by the collar on more than one occasion, just to have him go limp and flop in the dirt. Gravity seemed to favor his bulk. Once, Mom even tried out her new canister of pepper spray (no relation to Prissy's actual beau), catching Fred full in the face. He simply snorfed, shook his head, and pressed on like an aroused avalanche of saggy meat.

But as I said, Pepper was the winner in this genetic contest, and after only a couple of failed attempts, a litter quickened within the womb of Priscilla Jane Poodle. I distinctly remember the smell in my parents' bathroom after the puppies were born. It was vital and terrifying. I think there were five pups, though I really only remember two of them: the two that my sister named Bob and Nancy after my dad's parents. We managed to place most of the puppies right away, but Bob stayed with us longest. He went with us on our summer camping trip to Colorado, and we were pretty attached to him by the time Mom finally found him a home of his own.

Between the bother, expense, and disappointed children—not to mention the uninspiring profit margin—this was pretty much the end of Prissy's career as a breeder... and her next big adventure involved getting spayed. You can imagine that this provoked a number of questions with illuminating answers about biology, too.

During all of these various adventures and upheavals, Prudence suffered on the periphery. She avoided the puppies, the noise, the amorous packs of gentleman callers, and pretty much everyone in the house while still trying to maintain a semblance of ownership over as much of the domain as she could.

I remember asking if Prudence would ever have kittens, and Mom dodged the question at first. But eventually I learned that in her more fertile days Prudence had been the world's worst mother. Apparently, she would sneak off (as cats will do... loudly, just under one's window) and return home with a belly full of joy and erratic behavior, only to sneak off again and deposit her litter in some remote corner of our property. Not knowing what to do next, Prudence would then leave the new kittens wherever they dropped and forget about them. Mom told of finding feeble, nearly-dead kittens under bushes, in the tool shed, and even in the attic. She spoke tearfully of trying to save them and find them homes—only to have them succumb to the initial neglect and rejection of their mother.

The last straw was the day my Mom's mother came over and went out on the back patio to play the battered old piano that Dad had found somewhere. It was out of tune, of course, but one section of the keyboard seemed to be muted, and when the adults peered inside the machine they found six little kitten skeletons tangled in the hammer mechanism. The sentence for this crime: uterus removal.

Still, despite the cold, remorseless evil clearly dwelling in her soul, Prudence was a pleasant enough companion. I lost the battle for Prissy's affection early on; she didn't like coming up the stairs to my hot and messy room, and besides, she was too deeply devoted to Mom to leave her side. But Prudence roamed the house more widely, and she favored places that were Prissy-free, so I sometimes woke up with her curled peacefully on the foot of my bed. Of course, she being a cat, I was just as likely to wake up with her standing on my chest, working up a hairball, or catch her skulking into one of the closets in my room to leave unpleasant little treats that I would have to clean up.

While the bulk of their time was spent studiously ignoring each other, as Prissy and Prudence got older, they began to take pleasure in overtly annoying each other. Prissy, while never a big thinker, learned that Prudence liked to nap in certain places, and the dog began adjusting her navigational patterns so that she could appear as close as possible to the snoozing cat and nonchalantly poke her with her snout. The first few times I saw this happen, Prudence would launch herself up as if she'd been lanced with a hot needle, and backflip awkwardly over the arm of the couch in an amazing display of cat-fu. Once she popped herself nearly straight up and over the back of the couch in an artful parabolic arc, and when she didn't come back out right away, we peaked behind it to see her sitting regally, contemplating the wall under the big picture window as if that had been where she was sitting all along.

Gradually, Prudence learned to sleep more shallowly and became quite alert to any movement near her napping spots. Once she was conditioned to sense the approach, she couldn't be startled and she tried the always-reliable trick of ignoring her nemesis, patiently not reacting to the prodding. But that only emboldened Prissy, and if she got away with the first few pokes, she started adding a bark or two to her attack until Prudence had enough and responded with either a rousing chase around the living room, or a hasty exit from the house altogether.

Not willing to be a passive victim, Prudence began mounting surprise attacks of her own. One afternoon while I was changing the laundry, I spotted Prudence coming inside from what was probably an enjoyable morning of murdering birds and lizards. She seemed to be sauntering aimlessly across the family room, but when she reached the door to the main hallway, she reared back comically (like a cat version of Oliver Hardy) and darted into the kitchen instead. A few seconds later, Prissy came towards the kitchen from the hallway, clearly heading for her water bowl.

As the dog came around the corner, Prudence sprang out like a furry clawed Jack in the Box, and bopped Prissy on the nose. Prissy yelped in surprise and immediately gave chase. Prudence led her around the legs of the dining room table, back through the kitchen, and up the hallway to my sister's room. My sister's bed was a pedestal-style waterbed, with a cast iron headboard and footboard, and her lacy bedspread hung down to create a neat one-foot square runway all the way around the bed. By the time I got to the room, cat and dog had both slipped under the bedspread, and were doing laps around the bed at top speed.

Prudence, being slightly quicker, and a lot smarter, timed her exit perfectly. She reached the corner of the bed, and instead of continuing around the racetrack to the left, she made a right... just as she passed the post of the foot board. Prissy did not manage to make the same turn.

GONG!

By the time the dazed poodle regained her senses enough to extract herself from the tangle of lacy bedspread and walk in a straight line, Prudence was well out of reach on top of Mom's armoire, cleaning herself innocently as if she had been there all day.

At some point, Dad had installed flaps in the doors so the animals could let themselves in or out as they pleased. From the kitchen, there was one door to the garage, and another across the garage exiting to the side yard. This was generally convenient for everyone, but it did create several prime ambush points. I probably don't need to spell out the details—the cat was an expert at hiding where the dog would least expect it, and she had the patience to wait for the most opportune moment.

Eventually, my sister and I grew accustomed to this game, and we all got used to seeing Prudence settle in some out-of-the-way corner, nook, or cranny and just sit for hours, so we often didn't realize what she was up to until the trap was sprung and the chasing was over. For her part, Prissy had figured out that she needed to be on guard when going in or out through any of the door flaps. Even when Prudence was nowhere to be seen, Prissy would nudge the door two or three times before actually pushing through—and a few times, she actually worked herself into a paranoid fury, barking at the swinging flap and smacking it with a paw or her snout before deciding the cat was really elsewhere.

One morning, as I lingered over my bowl of cereal, I noticed something moving out the corner of my eye. In the entryway, Mom kept several bags of empty cereal boxes that were piled up, waiting to be sorted. She was an avid coupon-collector and always had brown grocery bags full of boxes with barcodes, coupons, promotional games, etc. Prudence's black tail extended out from between two of the bags—furred out with anticipation and twitching manically. On my way to the sink, I peeked between the bags, and saw that her attention was fixed on the door flap. Glancing over my shoulder, I could see that Prissy was out in the side yard, and headed for the door to come inside.

I didn't think about what I did next. I just casually leaned down and said, in a normal speaking voice, "Boo."

The cat's reaction was a thing of beauty. If I could take my camera phone back in time to capture one moment in the highest definition possible, this would be the moment. Prudence's legs pushed her up, farther up in the air than I had ever seen her go, and her body went rigid, with all four of her legs as fully extended as they could get. She somehow rotated in this completely stiffened state, like a taxidermist's model of a cat, white-eyed and staring at me in absolute terror as her body followed a parabola across the tiny foyer. She landed—nothing but net—tail first in one of the grocery bags full of discarded cardboard, and disappeared from view.

At that moment, Prissy poked a tentative nose through the door flap and gave a questioning "woof"—coincidentally, right at the bag where the terrorized cat had only just come to rest. This is the part that I wanted on film, because I swear that cat passed through the side of that bag at the molecular level. The bag was not torn, but Prudence, trailing a confetti of UPC symbols and scraps of paper, streaked out of the entryway at an altitude of between three and six inches, and we didn't see her for two days.

So, when I jump out at you from nowhere and can't stop laughing while you mutter angrily and try to put your skin back on, please don't take it personally. I learned this from my cat.

3
A Fatman and Thriller

Third grade was a banner year of badness for me. I had a horrid teacher who enjoyed humiliating the children who dared to be bored with her endless letter packets—and I learned the hard way that reading above grade level was no defense. But worse than annoying my teacher, my friends filled my head with dirty jokes.

"Rectum? Dang near killed 'em!"

"Ah, but one of these ladies is a cannibal!"

"Ma'am, I'm just making sure there ain't no BEES in this one!"

Since all I was learning in the public school seemed to be things better left between the covers of *Totally Gross Jokes #37*, my parents decided to send me to a private, Christian school.

Fourth grade was considered an "adjustment year." My teacher was an old classmate of my dad's—they had graduated from Grand Canyon College's teaching school, and they had decided to attribute all of my behavior problems to a need for discipline after the dismal failure of the public school teachers to provide any.

Fifth grade marked a change, though. My teacher that year was more nurturing, and encouraged my reading habits. Plus, I was no longer the freakish, unknown entity in the school; there were several, newer kids to take that title. And best of all, that was the year we were allowed to start Band, so for the first time I began making friends who shared a common, wholesome interest with me.

Of course, life wasn't perfect. Because there was Todd.

Todd was an unusually tall, broad, and blond fifth grader—a proto-jock whose body hadn't yet decided to be athletic or merely big. To my short, skinny eyes, he resembled a refrigerator, only one with a sneer and a unibrow where the freezer door should have been. For reasons lost in the mists of 1983, we took an instant dislike to each other. It didn't help that our names were so similar; teachers kept confusing us, and we were both offended by the confusion. We were also both offended that the other was offended... Well, you get the idea.

Todd took to taunting me whenever he passed me outside of class; "Tad the Retard" was his favorite refrain. He occasionally varied that with Christian-school insults like dummy, stupid, or, memorably, "tadpole," which he thought he'd invented. He considered those to be pretty brutal, but my skin had been thickened in the third grade by all of those *Totally Gross* jokes, and he quickly learned that verbal sparring was usually going to favor my quicker wit and saltier mouth—and I was agile enough to dodge the physical threats of his lumbering paws.

Teachers tried to intervene, telling us both to cool it, and I remember complaining to my mother about it. "They keep trying to make us act like friends, but he's just a big, fat bully!" Mom tried to tell me that bullies are usually insecure and just need friends. Sure he was new, but he seemed so large, impenetrably mean, and uninterested in being my friend. Plus, he was constantly surrounded by a gaggle of unapproachable football-throwing neandersmalls; so I took the less Christian but more satisfying strategy of making Todd's life miserable.

Little pranks—nothing harmful or damaging—began happening to Todd. Things would disappear from his desk and show up somewhere embarrassing (like the girls' bathroom). Drawings of Todd with dragging knuckles or a finger in his nose would fall out of his books. And I swear I didn't start it, but whenever he came near the table of fools I sat with at lunch, we could be heard singing, to the tune of the Adam West/Burt Ward *Batman* theme:

"Fatman! Da-da-da-da, da-da-da-da: Fatman!"

My friend Tony, who seemed so quiet and reserved when I first met him, blossomed into a fine cartoonist that year, thanks to the practice he got from drawing Fatman comics. The misadventures of Fatman and his rotating cadre of idiotic (usually fatally) sidekicks became an instant underground hit.

I barely noticed that Todd had mostly begun to leave me alone. He would scowl and barrel past me and my lunatic fringes, only occasionally serenading me if I passed his group's game of football as I walked to the Band room. One or two minutes of Todd singing "Tad is re-tard-ed!" seemed to justify weeks of serialized mischief on the cartoon pages, at least to my mind.

Sure, looking back, I can see that Todd had a pretty harsh year. The conflict was real, at first, but exaggerated in my immature brain. The damage we did to each other was (I hope) small; but it was only years later, when I was reliving all of the fun with Tony, that it occurred to me that I was... wrong.

I'd like to tell you there was some kind of satisfying climax to this conflict, but there never really was. Todd and I never fought... not with fists. Neither one of us attempted suicide, that I know of. There was no single moment when we said anything earth-shatteringly symbolic to each other. It was simply a matter of two idiot kids who didn't like each other jabbing each other with looks and catch-phrases, and wishing the other would drop dead.

So, if there's no point to this story, then why did I tell it? Well, I think maybe there's still something to be learned from this. A lot of my dear friends have made remarks about international issues that remind me quite a bit of the rift between Todd and Tad; one lumbering giant, and one self-important twat—neither one in the right. And yet, I'm supposed to be rooting for one of them to destroy the other just to prove that Evil shall not prevail!

I never destroyed my Big Enemy. Fatman never vanquished his nemesis, the Living Turd. We both imagined the other to be plotting something horrific for the other that never happened. And neither of us really got anything out of that ongoing conflict. I could have had all of my friends and their cartoons and the laughs *without* humiliating the other guy. He could have ended it all by simply ignoring me and my stupid jokes.

Instead, we made ourselves miserable, both feeling justified because the other was so... Evil.

Maybe we should have just sat down and talked... but we couldn't. We were young and stupid.

I spent three years in that Christian school, and to be brutally honest… it wasn't Christian enough for me! Once I was removed from the iniquitous influences of the Peoria Unified School District, I became very devout. I was Born Again at age 11, which made my family very proud, and I meant it. I was a True Believer, right down to my Holy socks, and it made me angry to see the other kids around me at this supposedly "Christian" school constantly reveling in everything Satan put out in the world to tempt them—slasher movies, raunchy TV shows, naughty magazines and books, and worst of all rock music!

I proudly listened only to Family Life Radio, where every night Dr. James Dobson would talk on *Focus on the Family* about the dangers of letting your children be exposed to harmful and worldly things. I took every word to heart.

You have to give me credit: I was genuinely worried about my classmates. I honestly believed that their souls were in jeopardy, and that they would end up running around campus with their pants down, setting fire to cars and buildings, doing drugs while they mutilated pets... Picture Bill Murray a la Ghostbusters: "Dogs and cats, living together… Mass hysteria!"

That was my fear.

And then came the field trip. One of the girls in my class was the daughter of an extremely wealthy construction mogul in the area, and he sponsored a field trip to his house for our class, complete with a fleet of limousines for the students. Looking back, this makes no sense; I have no idea what the educational value was in tramping about on his huge estate looking at his antique car collection and his enormous pool. But, there we were, and on the way back to the school, someone discovered the radio.

There were several of us in the car: my friends Robert and Scott, and the class bully, Todd. Upon discovering the controls for the radio, they promptly tuned in a Top 40 station. I protested. I grew increasingly incensed at the situation; not just that I didn't like the music, but that it was supposed to be a forbidden thing. I accused them all of loving Satan, and they just laughed.

Somehow I ended up pinned to the back seat by Scott, while Robert cranked the volume. "I love this song," he crowed. It was "Thriller." You have to understand that in my mind "Thriller" represented everything that was wrong with our society at that time. It was about zombies (the undead, a tool of Satan), it encouraged dancing (think "Church Lady"), and worst of all: Michael Jackson was a Jehovah's Witness!

Yeah, lame. But to me, sitting there as two of my best friends and my worst enemy laughed, taunted, and flaunted the Word of God, not to mention school rules, filled me with a righteous anger I had never felt before. I writhed and spat, I bucked and thrashed—all to no avail. No matter what I did, I was helpless to shut out the influence of Satan pouring from the speakers.

I was so mad that I leaned up and bit a chunk out of Scott's sternum.

In retrospect, it was extremely stupid, and for so many reasons. I understand now all the ways it was stupid, but until that happened, I didn't realize what a completely irrational dogmatic prick I was growing into.

I don't remember the aftermath. I don't remember being pulled out of the limo while teachers whisked Scott away to get his bite attended to. I don't remember my parents being called and waiting the half hour it took for them to arrive. I don't clearly remember the order of events or how I ended up in the principal's office. I do remember pleading my case, and trying to explain that I was defending my faith while the principal tried to hide the fact that he was laughing at me.

I do remember him patiently explaining to me that nothing, no matter how offensive it was to me personally, justified violence.

Receiving those four swats from the principal was a wake-up call. It certainly wasn't the point where I started questioning God (that wouldn't even be possible for me for at least another five years) but it was the point where I began to doubt myself. It was the point where I realized that being "saved" did not wrap one in a blanket of righteousness where I could do no wrong. It took me a while to absorb it all, but being humiliated forced me to accept some unpleasant realizations about myself. Eventually, I even grasped the fact that when it came to people like Todd, I was probably the real bully; and when it came to judging my friends, I needed to find better standards than the extremely unrealistic ones I was using.

I can still be an insufferable, self-righteous prick, but thanks to that experience I learned to watch for the danger signs. When I first discovered Socrates—"it is not in the nature of things that a bad man should injure one better than himself"—I thought back to the kid I was in that limo. A kid so sure that my attitude and actions were justified, that I could physically assault someone out of righteous rage.

I don't bite people anymore. It's not a very Christian thing to do, of course. But more importantly, it isn't moral.

I still don't really care much for Michael Jackson.

4
Call Me Maybe (Not)

My father was a firefighter. He had tried his hand at teaching, but it simply hadn't suited him. He had no patience for dealing with saucy high school students in the 1969 version of Glendale, Arizona, so after only one year, he took a position in the Phoenix Fire Department.

He started when I was extremely little, so all I remember growing up was the natural pattern of having Daddy home two days and at work on the third. One 24-hour shift every three days isn't a bad deal, but as we got to that age where we began to notice he was gone, Mom started the tradition of calling him at bedtime.

You know how those calls go; the kid is whiny and tired but doesn't want to sleep, and you put him on the phone so he starts to perform. My sister and I would make goony noises and tell Dad lame jokes, and he would tell us exciting tales from the firehouse ("Tonight, Fred tried to make chili and set fire to the cooktop!"). We dragged it out as long as possible, and Mom would try to hurry us up. Every call ended the same way:

"Love you!" And a big, loud kiss—MWAH!

These routine phone calls tapered off, as they do when kids get a little older. I still loved talking to Dad, but the phone itself wasn't that exciting, and I knew he was going to be home the next day. My sister was four years behind me though, so when I had begun to outgrow the bedtime phone calls, she was just getting into it. She would remind Mom to call, or we would fight over who got to dial, then she would chatter at him until it was my turn to say good night, all rounded out with the obligatory, "Love you! MWAH!"

The only other times we were on the phone tended to be special occasions like birthdays or Christmas, and it was usually talking to a grandma or a grandpa. These were exciting events, because Mom's folks traveled around a lot, and we didn't get to see them often. We would blather on at them about whatever we were doing in our solipsistic lives, and Grandma would cluck about the expensive long distance charges, and then eventually... "Love you! MWAH!"

Sometimes it would be Dad's folks calling for a birthday; or Aunt Ginny out in Florida; or (even more rarely) the relatives in New Jersey. I don't remember a whole lot about specifics, but you know how I ramble on trying to be amusing, and I'm pretty sure that's what I was like then, too—so I'm sure I told stories ranging from hilarious to awkward, mumbled about school and loving Jesus, and passed the phone to my sister before we ended with that habitual, "Love you! MWAH!"

But seasons turn, the tides roll in and out, and kids outgrow the easy sharing of casual emotion, and somewhere around the point when my age hit double digits, I started dodging the phone calls as much as possible. I'd still get dragged to the phone for certain annual rituals, but it wasn't what you'd call an everyday sort of tool.

Then one day, the phone rang, and my mom called me downstairs (because it was, you know, stuck to the wall down there), and Scott from school was speaking to me. This was odd. No one from school had ever called me before, and Scott and I had never been the closest of friends. He was asking me over to play at the park near his house. I was so very confused, I remember trying to hand the phone back to Mom for her to deal with it. Of course, since we lived 15 miles from the school, and my classmates almost all lived in the neighborhoods immediately surrounding it, Mom wasn't about to take me anywhere on a whim like that—so I think I thanked him for asking, but had to turn him down.

And that's where my relationship with the phone kind of started out: a mixture of that grudgingly dutiful family feeling with an extra dose of bafflement and sad confusion.

A couple of years after Scott's call, I had switched schools, and I was now at the age where most of my peers spent a great deal more time on the phone. I didn't, but that was about to change thanks to a special group assignment for science class. We were paired up with partners, and we were instructed to get together to build a model of the solar system. I brought home a phone number for my friend and classmate, Tony (of Fatman fame).

I was pretty excited about working on a project with another kid. Living so far away from the world, we really didn't get a lot of spontaneous play time with anyone outside of our church (and it was a small church, so kids my own age were a rarity). I liked Tony, so I was looking forward to hanging out with him. But something had to happen first. Something I hadn't ever really done before.

I had to call him.

The memory of making the phone call is pretty clear—I can still see the spinning plastic dial, and hear the static-shrouded clicks of the rotor. I can remember the details of all the things sitting on Mom's dresser in front of me as I waited for someone to pick up, and then as I croaked my well-rehearsed greeting. (Mom had to coach me thoroughly on phone etiquette, you know: say "Hello," and tell them your name, then ask for the person you're calling.) Once I got Tony on the line, it kind of clicked. This was normal. It was just talking! I can do that —no problem! We made our plans, set times, confirmed our transportation arrangements and agreed on materials. Before I knew it, we were all set.

"Alright, see you Saturday. Love you! MWAH!"

Wait. What? What the... actual... Did I just blow a big, loud kiss at my classmate over the phone?

Yes. Yes, I did.

I think Mom laughed the whole rest of that week, and she may have still been giggling when she dropped me off that Saturday at Tony's house. I was mortified, and not looking forward to this anymore. But I had nothing to worry about. Tony hadn't even noticed. He had been so nervous about being on the phone, he'd hung up when I said, "Alright..."

Still—this was such a harsh entry into the world of teenaged telecommunications. At least I learned the ever-valuable Lesson #1: No big, loud kissing.

5
A Pinch of Nerve

"I look so cool," the boy thought, as he checked out his image in the bathroom mirror.

Black shoes, black slacks. Turquoise shirt with silver braid glued around the cuffs. The key piece, and the item he was most proud of, was the Starfleet badge he had fashioned from cardboard and masking tape and covered in gold paint. His hair was plastered down with the black hairspray his mom had picked up at the costume shop—the sole item he had needed to purchase to make his costume complete. Except for the ears. No one in Arizona sold pointed ears; at least not that a seventh grader could afford for a mere Halloween costume.

Taking one last long, admiring look, he wiped the smile from his face, arched an eyebrow, and froze his expression into a cool, appraising blankness. The boy was gone, and Mr. Spock stepped out of the bathroom.

Spock strode to the boy's desk, and picked up his tricorder (which said "Panasonic" on the side, and held a cassette of pre-recorded sound effects lovingly recorded off of the small TV set in the boy's room). He clipped his phaser (Legos, wrapped in masking tape, and painted) to his belt, and beamed himself downstairs to the waiting Datsun shuttle in the garage.

The pilot and other passenger—the boy's mother and sister, Snow White—chattered excitedly about the Halloween party at the school. Spock answered them with a crisp "Yes," "No," or "Fascinating," as the social situation required, but otherwise gazed analytically out the window. He breathed deeply, and used ancient Vulcan meditation techniques to control human emotions—Anticipation! Excitement!—that threatened to surge and break his carefully cultivated character.

The shuttle docked in the front lot, and the landing party approached the entrance to the carnival. Mom—the pilot, rather—bought tickets for the games and divided them between Spock and Snow White, and he thanked her briskly before turning on his heel and striding off to observe the local population's harvest rites.

He noted the knotted clusters of friends: females clinging and giggling in groups of five or six, and males lurking and sulking in smaller groups. The costumes chosen seemed to follow a theme also along gender lines: girls varied between younger pastel princesses and older rock goddesses while boys favored gore-spattered corpses or favorite movie characters.

A grubby boy, painted green and wearing a cardboard box on his back, broke off from one of the small clusters and approached Spock. "What are you s'posed to be?" he demanded.

"I am Commander Spock of the Federation Starship Enterprise," Spock replied. He raised his eyebrow. "May I inquire as to your identity?"

"I'm Michelangelo," the other boy said, brandishing a pair of plastic nunchuks. "Kevin was supposed to be Donatello, but he decided we'd look like we were a couple if we were both Ninja Turtles. So he's a vampire." He gestured toward a boy who seemed to be dressed normally, except for eye makeup and uncomfortable-looking plastic fangs. "Wanna check out the cakewalk?"

"I will merely observe," Spock said.

The turtle boy—whose name was actually Larry—won the cake. He, Spock, and Kevin the vampire began wandering past the music building toward the area set aside for rides. Spock excused himself to use the sanitation facility. When he came back out, his companions were nowhere to be found.

The boy—no, Spock—forced down panicky emotions and assessed the situation coolly. There was no need to feel abandoned, as he was here to learn the native customs and evaluate these people for membership in the Federation. He would continue his investigation alone.

Not quite alone. A voluptuous animal with long, furry ears and an adorable little nose mask (adorned with whiskers that only accentuated the sprinkle of freckles across her cheeks) hopped in front of him. A brown leotard with a fluffy tail pinned to the back completed the bunny costume of Loree VanDorn. Spock nearly melted away completely, leaving the boy to gibber self-consciously on the sidewalk, but he resisted the feverish haze of hormones long enough to take another deep breath.

"Hello, Loree," he said. The bunny grinned back at him.

"So, what are you supposed to be? Dr. Spock?" she chirped.

He sighed. "No, actually. Dr. Spock is the child-rearing expert. I am *Commander* Spock, of the Starship Enterprise."

"Okay," she sighed, rolling her eyes. "Did you want to go to the cafeteria? They're having a dance in there."

Spock's vision blurred at the prospect of dancing with a bunny version of Loree VanDorn, but before he could reply, there was a commotion behind the music building. Shrieks of indignation and loud, whooping laughter preceded a Ninja Turtle, a vampire, and a hail of flying chunks of cake. They ran up to Spock and nearly collapsed in hysterics.

"Omigod, omigod, omigod! Julie Hunt was back there..." one began.

"...with Bobby Sweet, and they were..." the other continued.

"...going to do *it*!"

"No, they weren't! They were just kissing!"

"She had her costume off!"

"Just the mask!"

"No, they were gonna go all the way!"

"But she wouldn't..."

"She would too... she's a total flooze..."

"No, way! She's so tight she squeaks..."

"Well, if you hadn't thrown the cake at 'em..."

Loree's face had turned hard and cold. "Julie's my friend, you jerks." She cast a baleful glare at Spock, and turned to go find her friend. Spock watched her go, mouth hanging slightly open. He had been so close...

"...you shoulda seen her face!" Larry was saying. "It was so *funny*!"

"I need to go," Spock said, and turned to follow the huffy rabbit—

—and ran straight into an angry wall of cake-covered football jersey. He looked up into the red, sweating face of Bobby Sweet, known in gym class as Bobby Sweat. Bobby glared down at him and took note of the cowering pair behind him. Larry and Kevin were already poised for flight, and took off headlong when Bobby grabbed Spock's arm.

The pain in Spock's arm focused his attention away from his emotions, and Spock spoke to the seething adolescent in front of him: "Your anger is not logical. It was not I who covered you with pastry."

"Stuff it, geek-boy," growled the angry boy in the soiled Roger Staubach jersey. "You're their friend, so you're going down, too!" His voice broke awkwardly but that stole none of the menace from his threat. Spock snaked his free arm upward, and reached for the pressure point in Bobby's neck to deliver a Vulcan nerve pinch. His fingers pressed into solid, ungiving steel.

"Are you wearing shoulder pads?" Spock asked, re-thinking his tactics.

"Nope," said Bobby, drawing back his fist.

Spock's mind raced. There was no logical counter-argument to the bigger boy's rage. He knew, intellectually, that species existed who did not share his distaste for violence, and when confronted with a member of one such species, prudence called for a surgical strike and

31

rapid retreat. This situation required the unexpected. Spock bowed his head and let the boy inside him take over.

With his eyes cast down, the boy saw an opening, and he quickly looked back up, giving his opponent a small grin that made the rising fist waver. The boy lowered his hand from its futile grip on the bull-like neck, and with his fingers still forming the position for the painful Vulcan Death Grip, he asked about another standard piece of football equipment: "Cup?"

It was a gamble, but the boy jabbed his Death Grip downward, and Bobby's eyes gave him the answer by widening in surprise and pain. The grip on the boy's arm loosened and he dove out of reach and started running, leaving logic behind on the wind, along with a peal of his own triumphant laughter.

The boy stopped when he felt he was safely away, and turned to make sure he wasn't being pursued. He wasn't. Bobby was coiled around the pain in the center of his being, and Julie had appeared from somewhere to console him. Loree was by Julie's side, and glaring photon torpedoes back at Mr. Spock. The passing crowd was either staring at him with shock, or ignoring him completely. No one seemed impressed with his handling of the situation.

He spotted his friends-by-default, the Ninja Turtle and vampire, and headed their way to seek camaraderie, and perhaps their thanks for his quick thinking.

"Nice grab," they sneered. "Jealous of Julie?" They howled with laughter, heaping more abuse on him as they collapsed against each other with mirth, both denigrating his combat prowess and questioning his sexual orientation. He felt his face flush, and the heat of building tears pressed against his eyes; but then Spock returned, slowly.

He mustered what remained of his dignity, straightened his posture, and clasped his hands behind his back. "You," he said, "are *highly* illogical!"

And with that, Mr. Spock turned his back on the crowd, and stalked off; the only one surprised at the unrepentant fickleness of middle-schoolers.

6
Nemeses

I sat astride my bicycle at the crest of Suicide Hill, staring down at its two wicked 90-degree dog legs. My cousin Aaron was behind me, still recovering from riding up the incline on his BMX dirt bike by taking great, whooping gasps of breath. My bike was a 10-speed street bike, and I knew how to use my gears to get up a hill.

Anyone from a part of the world that had real hills would laugh at us for even calling this knob of wind-blasted volcanic debris a "hill," but it was all we had. It jutted out of the otherwise flat desert and was bisected by a paved bit of road perpendicular to Beardsley Boulevard, which climbed the south side of the hill into a cleft between the two low summits. They topped out at maybe 300 feet, though the crest we sat on wasn't even that high. Still, we could see across the rooftops of the approaching suburban developments, and we could see down that steep length of blacktop—which is what we had come to conquer.

I kicked off abruptly, catching Aaron mid-wisecrack, and I heard his voice cut off in surprise at my unexpected courage just before the rising wind past my ears would have drowned him out anyway. I felt a sound coming up from my chest that alternated between exhilaration and terror, but I was too busy leaning into first one turn, then the next, to pay attention to any non-essential details.

Aaron had not waited for me to come to a full stop before he started down. I was just turning to shout, "Come on, nerd, what are you waiting for?" when I saw him wreck. The sight was spectacular. He took the first turn too sharply, waited a hair too long to correct, and skidded just enough for his back tire to touch the gravel at the side of the road. From my point of view, his bike leapt sideways into the air, over the drop-off, tipping and spinning in a gyroscope of boy, rubber, and metal… before tumbling into the inhospitable tangle of weeds, prickers, cactus, and rocks below.

I pedaled back up toward where Aaron had gone over to make sure he was okay, and by the time I got there, he had extricated himself and his BMX from the worst of it. He pushed his bike toward me with one hand, and held his other arm so he could survey what looked like raw hamburger studded with a variety of sharp and unpleasant foreign matter.

"I guess I'll need the tweezers again," he sighed. But he quickly brightened and said, "This will make a rad scab for my collection!"

Aaron was two years younger than me, but he was clearly able to take more damage than I ever could. As a rule, he was quicker, more athletic, and aside from this moment, less prone to accidents than I was. He was also far more durable when they occurred. He had a BMX because he raced competitively; he played soccer in a league; and he even rode skateboards—which kept him covered in scabs he collected in a cardboard box (please, don't ask me why). These were all things that were neither available nor desirable to me. I was older, more cautious, and much more well-read. We had an odd relationship that seemed to combine mutual respect with baffled pity for each other's failings—but it worked.

This particular adventure was possible because my parents had decided that I could handle riding my bike the seven miles to Aaron's house. The route took me down long orchard roads, through an old vineyard, and past a new golf course bordering several new housing developments. Suicide Hill was only a half mile north of his house, and our church was only two miles east of that.

Until I had earned the freedom to bike to his house, church had been the only place I saw Aaron, aside from family gatherings around birthdays and holidays. My aunt liked to have me around because I exerted a calming influence. When I would visit, she had an excuse to drive away the neighborhood skate punks who came calling for Aaron, and she could relax knowing that I would keep her son out of trouble.

When we were in church I demonstrated an ability to quiet Aaron during the sermons, and sometimes even got him to read the Bible! The secret behind that trick was that I had been reading the Bible on my own for years, and I knew where all of the really *good* stories were. I knew how to find the parts that were apparently written by Stephen King. I would slip him 2 Kings chapter 9, and while he read about Jehu riding into Jezreel to have Jezebel chucked off a balcony, I looked up Judges 4 in another copy. When he was done reading about Jezebel's splattery end, we'd swap Bibles and he'd read all about Jael driving a tent peg through Sisera's head. Then, I'd have him flip back a chapter to read about Ehud burying a cubit-long sword in the belly fat of King Eglon. When violence got boring, there was always the Song of Solomon, with its baffling comparisons of women's anatomy to various fruits and vegetables.

And verily, the people of the congregation did marvel at our fervor for the Word of the Lord.

My schoolmates were much less impressed with my fervor. By this point, I had been placed back in the public schools. My dad figured that there was no point in paying the extra tuition for me to learn to bite people over Michael Jackson songs. He probably had a point, but I missed Tony and my other friends and didn't have much in common with anyone from Pioneer Elementary after three years of absence.

We didn't have what some parts of the country refer to as junior high school or middle school, but this year of transition happened during the equivalent of those grades. And as many a parent of middle-grade students will tell you: middle school is when children are at their worst with interpersonal relationships. It's easy to look back and catalog my mistakes, but at the time, I couldn't figure out why I was so hated and so lonely.

I could blame my religion for this, but I wasn't the only religious kid at the school. Sure, I took fellow students to task for trying to convince me that evolution was real, and I had a tendency to give anyone who tried to talk to me about horror movies or rock music an earful of moral indignation—but those were never the things that seemed to bother people. There were disagreements in class over the course material, and squabbles over rules on the playground. Some kids just seemed to form an instant dislike for no discernable reason, and we would spit insults at each other with no provocation.

One kid from that latter group was named Andy; he was the first of many doppelgangers in my life. There have been a number of people over the years that others have sworn bore a close resemblance to me. Andy and I were of similar builds, had similar haircuts, and even (much to our mutual disgust) owned identical striped polo shirts—which we discovered when we both wore our matching shirts to school on the same day.

I didn't really have anything against Andy, but he was aspiring to be a Cool Kid, and I was an inconvenient and unworthy competitor for that title in his mind. I didn't react well to his put-downs. He was more original than Todd had been in fourth grade, but I've never been one to withhold a withering comeback, and it didn't take long for me to turn Andy into a bitter enemy. It was a short trip from loathing Andy to lashing out at anyone who compared the two of us.

(Jesus Christ—I just got out a yearbook, and even now I can see *he looked just like me!*)

It was during this time that I became more than a little obsessed with a popular television series about invading aliens disguised as human beings—or *V*, for those of you in the know.

I was never allowed to watch *V*, but it was the so-called "water-cooler" show that year. All of the kids who were watching it would talk about it in the lunchroom, and I would avidly listen for details. The plot points and characters were completely baffling to me by the time the story had been filtered through the barely articulate prepubescent lens of my classmates, but somehow, I became convinced that I actually was a "V."

The conceit played to both my sense of isolation at school, and my sense of being special at home and church. Being an alien walking around in human disguise was more than the perfect metaphor for feeling both rejected as well as chosen—the apparent contradiction made perfect sense if I realized I was no earthling, but something better, smarter, and more terrifying. The whole notion got mixed up with my understanding of what faith was in a way that was impossible for me to articulate to anyone, without sounding crazy.

I know because I tried to talk to my sister and to my cousin Aaron, and they told me I sounded crazy. I once tried to tell my dad about it, but there were some extenuating circumstances that made that conversation impossible. Our house was directly under the flight path for Luke Air Force Base, and I had already come gibbering to my parents' bedroom in terror of the sight of weird lights in the sky. I'm sure when I started in about lizard aliens disguised as people, Dad just figured it was part of my imaginary UFO shenanigans.

I didn't exactly have a confidant at school to try to discuss this with, but I did have a tendency to let my mind wander in classes where I had already finished the material, and I said or did odd things while in my own little world. The other kids picked up on some of it. Andy had a few choice sanity-based insults. And as others butted up against my weird mix of imagination, bombast, and self-assurance, I cultivated a few more nemeses. Between the atheist kid I scorned for his evolutionary ideas and the Mormons I mocked for their crazy beliefs, I found myself surrounded by exasperated rivals who had no idea why I was fighting them so passionately.

The same logic I used to defend my faith could be employed by the Mormons to defend their nonsensical myths—and the same skepticism I brought to bear on their myths seemed to undermine my own claims and assertions. Identifying as an alien opened up a gulf in my reality that left me defenseless against my own dumb obsession. I spent a growing amount of energy just dealing with the cognitive dissonance of ignoring how much of my worldview consisted of antagonistic bullshit.

At least I still had Aaron. His parents were both working a lot of night shifts, so they started turning up at church less reliably, but when he was there, he was like a balm to me. Of course, he was entering that awful middle school stage of life, too. As he matured and grew into being a popular kid at his school, he picked up on my own decline. He grew less tolerant of my fussy attempts to reel in his behavior, so our time together after church usually devolved into chasing, taunting, and other kinds of mayhem.

Our little church had been struggling to raise funds for a real congregation building for several years by that point, and the building committee had finally scraped together enough to break ground and lay a concrete foundation. This meant that behind the semi-permanent structure of the double-wide trailer we had been meeting in, there was now a deceptively dangerous place out of sight of the adults, where we were not supposed to go. The torn-up piles of dirt, discarded construction materials, and the menacing spikes of rebar were too strong of an attraction for Aaron, though, and more often than not, I found myself in trouble for trying to catch him and drag him back to where we were supposed to be.

To give the youth group something to do while adults visited between services, someone installed a basketball hoop at one end of the parking lot. This worked for a brief time, but Aaron bored of defeating me at every variation of Horse and one-on-one we knew. He found it hilarious to challenge me to a free-throw duel, then run off into the construction debris and start flinging dirt clods at me which burst on the ground like bombs. I tried chasing him, only to get yelled at for running by the foundation; I tried ignoring him, only to get yelled at for letting him pepper the new blacktop of the parking lot with dirt.

One Sunday evening, in a particularly dark mood, Aaron slipped off into the growing gloom and started launching dirt clods again. I tried to ignore him, I snapped at him angrily, and finally, I grew so furious, I began throwing back whatever I could find.

"Hey!" he shouted at me out of the dark. "You threw a rock!"

"Well, if you don't like it, quit being a jerk and come back over here!"

His answer sailed out of the night, just over my head and bounced under Brother Ernie's battered old Ford. It was a rock the size of an egg, and I lost my mind.

I dove for the decorative gravel by the church's front door, and with all of the adults inside, not watching us, I launched a barrage of rocks and mild curses at my cousin in the dark. He easily avoided my terribly mis-timed and mis-aimed missiles by running back and forth between bushes and mounds of dirt. I was so angry, I channeled all of my rage and frustration—at Andy, at the atheists, at the Mormons, at being a secret space alien, at not being taken seriously—and when I ran out of things to throw, I looked up to see Aaron's answer spinning toward me out of the dark.

The rock tumbled slowly through the air, and entered the cone of light from the spotlight on the wall of the church. I watched it approach in fascination, not entirely grasping what it was or where it was going, despite having just unloaded an armful of the things myself. I could not move. I could not dodge.

The bridge of my nose became a very bright, very heavy piece of my face just then. The point of impact seemed to illuminate the entire inside of my skull, and I felt myself turn and fall onto my hands and knees next to someone's car. I didn't feel like I was reacting to being hit in the face with a rock as much as I felt like my face was being pulled insistently down so the blacktop could tell me a secret. If this was a fraction of what the Biblical practice of stoning felt like, I was going to have to re-read some of the passages with this new perspective.

I think I recovered my senses rather quickly, and the brightness and heaviness coalesced into a single dark point of pain just under my left eye. I became aware of Aaron, wringing his hands together and pacing around me chanting, "Ohshit, ohshit, ohsit," as he tried to determine whether he had killed me.

"You," I told him, "are one stupid fucker."

That seemed to reassure him. He didn't call me out on using that word until years later, when we were grown up and reminiscing. Instead, he breathed out a sigh of relief, and ran inside to get help.

Later, sitting quietly with my dad as he applied an ice pack to what would turn into a wicked shiner with a hard, rock-sized hematoma, I lied about what had happened. Dad let me spin some stupid excuse about accidentally leaning in too close to the car door in the dark, and opening the door on my face. He didn't challenge my story, because he knew perfectly well what had happened, but he also knew that Aaron was falling all over himself with remorse and dread of whatever punishment he was likely to receive. He also knew that I knew that I had done wrong, and that I wasn't going to repeat that mistake.

Of all the lectures I had heard about Doing Unto Others and Reaping What One Sows, nothing had ever served to illustrate the point of the Golden Rule like that stone in the night. A stone that I had not thrown, but that I was responsible for. I wasn't likely to forget what that stone had taught me about karma and tolerance, even if it would take another two decades for the lesson to sink in.

Aaron waited for a chance to approach when there wouldn't be anyone around to hear him. "I'm sorry," he said. "Thanks for not ratting me out."

"It doesn't hurt that bad," I said. It was true. Maybe I was more durable than I thought.

"At least now you know," he said, with a teasing note in his voice.

"Know what?"

"You know you're not a lizard under your skin."

7
The Monkee

The first real social engagement I attended was the homecoming dance my freshman year of high school. My parents felt that raising a family 15 miles from the rest of the world was great for keeping us protected from corrupting influences, while still keeping us close enough to the real city for things like "food" and "health care." So when I went to my first dance, I was socially backward and totally unprepared for what was about to happen to me.

I went to the dance alone, though that wasn't my original plan. I had asked one girl (I think her name was Cheryl) upon whom I had developed a minor crush, and from this perspective twenty years later, it's hard to remember exactly what her reaction was. I think it was best described as polite, but definitely not interested.

But there I was, watching large children pretend to be small adults in the dim lighting. The cafeteria had streamers, mirror-balls, laser lights, and a DJ playing all of the hottest hits of the day: RunDMC, Aerosmith, Chris de Burgh, and... the Monkees. For those who don't know, the Monkees were a band from the 1960s that were assembled by some record and TV producers to capitalize on Beatlemania. Mom had one of their records, which I had all but memorized, and the TV series had entered syndication as part of the mid-1980s nostalgia movement for all things 60s.

As I wandered the periphery of the dancing horde, I heard a small voice from somewhere behind and below me say, "Would you like to dance?"

I couldn't see very well, but there was someone female down there—shorter than even me!—and so I agreed. We wandered out onto the floor just in time for a slow dance: the Monkees' "I Wanna Be Free." As Davy Jones crooned to us, my anonymous partner chattered excitedly. I couldn't really hear much, but I did catch that she really, *really* loved the Monkees.

At some point, my habit of singing or humming along with whatever music was in the area when I'm bored apparently took over. She gazed up at me, utterly smitten and asked, "Do you like the Monkees, too?"

I nodded. "Yeah, they're pretty cool." What did I know about cool?

That really should have been it—a geeky but pleasant social experience. Put it in your diary, and seal it away to reflect on twenty years later. But come Monday...

Band was first hour, and afterwards I had to head across campus to Algebra, with a stop at the large bank of lockers midway. When I slammed my door shut, there was a small simian face framed by a frizzy blonde Brillo pad and bristling with braces and zits. I couldn't guess at the gender, let alone the identity. It wore a Monkees tee-shirt the way most kids were wearing Def Leppard or Van Halen tees, and it peeped happily up at me, "Hi, sweetie!" Everyone whirled and stared, and I tried to vanish into my locker.

If the problem here had merely a matter of realizing the mysterious girl from the darkened dance floor was super-dorky in the daylight, and that all I had to do was look beneath the surface to find a heart of gold, this would be a different story. Instead, I was face to face with someone whose only adventure with hygiene had apparently been the night of the dance. And this was only the superficial reaction of "dancer's remorse." Things became painfully awkward over the following weeks as I tried to extricate myself from the Monkee's orbit.

The teasing of my classmates wasn't what bothered me. Sure, I was uncomfortably attuned to the fact that I was probably only reacting to the Monkee the way Cheryl had reacted to me, inviting an uncomfortable comparison between my unwanted advances and those of the Monkee. But the guilt I felt at making someone else experience that quickly evaporated into desperation as the Monkee's behavior proved to be increasingly erratic and disturbing.

The truism that "kids can be cruel" did not include the sorts of ambushes she launched on other girls in the school. Had she gone after the hip crowd, her actions would have made some sense in the age of John Hughes movies about popular kids and outcasts. But her targets tended to be random, and her attacks verged on being unhinged. She would spot me crossing the campus, run over excitedly, and then stop mid-stride to scream at someone across the quad. There was no discernable provocation. Just sudden and frightening outbursts.

I tried not to be mean, but I felt like I was stuck to a glue trap. That private agony of not wanting to hurt her feelings melted into a rather pathetic need to escape, which she picked up on and seemed to find unattractive. When she stopped paying attention to me, I was perfectly content to fade back into the background of her story.

As fate would have it, I was supplanted in her affections by a new kid who transferred from across town over the holidays, and theirs became a storied and lurid romance. His name was Burt, and he was the very model of dorkiness. Of course, everyone who had noticed her earlier crush on me made sure to point out that I had been tossed aside for his sake. Kids can be cruel, as you may know.

Burt's adventures were legion. He was like a nerd version of Don Quixote; he had no idea that he was neither liked nor respected, yet he behaved as though he were the hero of an epic high school story. He constantly found new ways to draw attention to himself, and no matter how embarrassing the situation, he reveled in that attention.

Somehow, Burt learned that his girlfriend had been following me around before his arrival, and he made it his mission to demonstrate his superiority to me. We were in the same History class, and if I answered a question or made a joke, he had to respond—usually with an awkward not-joke that left most of us puzzled. Once, he made himself laugh so hard, he blew an enormous snot into the hair of the cheerleader sitting a row ahead of him.

It got worse for a time when he tried to join the choir. Band and Choir had always been my safe areas—Band because I was a quintessential band geek, and Choir because I had learned early on that it was a socially acceptable way to spend time with girls without having to contend with alpha males spoiling everything with their testosterone and machismo.

Burt decided he was going to be the Choir Alpha—with hilarious results, since he couldn't sing. Between his boorish antics, his honking assault of a voice, and his inability to learn the music, he didn't last long. He was with us for one semester, long enough to ruin a third of a concert (with his Monkee love in the audience, gazing adoringly up at him), and then the troubles started.

The torrid break up of Burt and the Monkee rocked the entire school. They began squabbling openly between classes and when they encountered each other in the courtyard before and after school. Sinister looks, insults both hissed and shouted, and a memorable eruption of violence one afternoon when Burt lost his temper and smashed a locker, earning him a transfer to yet another school. I bore the relatively minor embarrassment of having those who remembered her earlier infatuation with me speculate out loud about whether she and I would reunite, and I kept my distance and hoped it wouldn't come to that.

But then, she disappeared. She simply stopped showing up at school, and her even newer boyfriend refused to comment on where she went (though he did enjoy a perverse kind of celebrity as the rumors flew around the school). When it became apparent that she had not done away with herself or pined away for lack of my sophomoric affections, I put her out of my mind.

The next year, her sister showed up. The sister had some issues herself; she was blind, and had two glass eyes which she loved to take out and use in practical jokes. She rolled the eyes back and forth on her desk in class, waiting for the teacher to work up nerve to say something to her. Or she would stand around the corner from people, extend one eye around the corner with her fingers and say, "I seeeeee *you*!!" in a haunting, sing-song voice.

At some point, I ended up talking to the sister and decided to ask where the Monkee had disappeared to. It was meant to be an airy, nonchalant kind of question. The answer was neither airy nor nonchalant. She was in jail for molesting some kids she was babysitting.

After the sister told me this, she shrugged and headed to her next class, leaving me to ponder how all of the awful things that high schoolers do and say to each other might affect us, and wondering if I had anything to do with the Monkee's downfall. I couldn't have known that she had it in her to do something like that, and yet, the news hadn't truly surprised me. This fact fell in with all of those vague alarms and red flags, and justified my initial reaction to her that first Monday after the dance.

My run-in with the Monkee left me feeling alone in a way that I hadn't experienced before. The mad loneliness of middle school had been about making friends; yet now, I had some friends in high school. But coming into such close contact with someone so damaged left me wondering if I wasn't too damaged to find someone to love. At best, if I were to find someone who liked me, I had a new worry:

Would I ever appeal to anyone who wasn't out of her mind?

8

Virgin Oil, or, The Fat's Out of the Bag

I haven't always been the calm, self-assured celebrity you see before you. In fact, I'm not now. But that's beside the point: I'm here to tell you how it all began. My big break, my discovery...

Cactus High School was the nearest school to us, and it was 15 miles away along with everything else in the city. My parents were not poor; they were frugal. When I got to that certain, magical age, I wanted a car to drive myself to school. Funnily enough, my parents didn't want to continue chauffeuring me, either, so in that sense our wishes aligned. But car insurance for a 16-year-old boy is astronomically high. So my father determined that I should pay my own insurance. And, in order to pay for insurance, I needed a job.

QED.

Since I had a pretty full after-school schedule between Band, Choir, and theater productions, I had a difficult time finding the right job.

Then one day, I noticed that one of my fellow Band geeks was working behind the serving lines in the cafeteria. This sort of job couldn't exist in public schools now, I'm sure, thanks to contracts and other legal issues, but in the 1980s it was a great opportunity to invest an hour a day, and pick up a free meal and some pocket money. The cafeteria didn't pay much, but it was enough to make my dad happy.

The job didn't start out very glamorously. I was a dismal failure at kitchen duty. At home, when Mom had asked me to help, I'd have a few clatters, a couple of knife drops, and a little broken glass; she invariably told me the same thing as she bent to collect the pieces of a set of heirloom glassware: "Go tell your father he wants you." But a school cafeteria's cookware is very durable and can survive quite a bit of abuse from a klutzy high-schooler, so with a bit of persistence, patience, and a smidgen of yelling, I got the hang of things.

After a short while, I even found my Niche, my Place in the Universe, my Special Purpose: they made me the Fry Guy.

The task was simple: put the French fries into the paper bowls and hand them out. Somehow this tiny bit of social interaction brought out the showman in me. I discovered, welling from deep within my bosom, this amazing gift of repartee! I found one thousand ways to say, "Would you like fries with that?" and provoke a giggle. My portions became famous ("Dude, he really piled them on!") and my delivery became as polished as the reachable sections of the Blarney Stone.

My God, it was a wonderful time that I looked forward to each day. Girls smiled at me! Guys did that super-cool head-nod thing (and refrained from threatening me with bodily harm). By and large, my classmates—most of whom wouldn't have dignified me with their loathing if I had asked for it—actually liked to be served by me. I became a minor high school celebrity. The Fry Guy. With capital letters!

This position of respect led to a few new skills as well. The boss-lady let me operate the fryer, and I learned the importance of keeping clean, fresh oil heated to just the right temperature. I learned the exact right amount of time to leave the fries down and how long they would need to drain before serving them up.

Not only did I have insurance money, respect, and a future in the food services, I had fun. I learned that my generally optimistic attitude was both rare and desirable. By volunteering for the seemingly mundane task of washing up, I was rewarded by getting asked to do really prestigious jobs, like washing out the 50-gallon cookpot on chili or beef stew days. (You haven't lived until you've sung "I Am the Pirate King" from inside a suds-filled cauldron. It is, it is a glorious thing!) Truly, I had arrived.

One fine day, riding on a cresting wave of popularity, and feeling on top of the world as I handed out perfectly crisped and golden potato strings to my fans and admirers, a cloud crossed over the sun. A sulky blonde-haired girl came through the line and glumly took a basket of my now-famous fries... but she didn't smile. I made some witty remark—I'm sure it was *very* suave and tasteful—and instead of warming to my charm, she stared into my face with widening eyes, dropped her tray and rushed out of the cafeteria line at a near run.

I shrugged it off; every comedian has to learn to deal with hecklers. No biggie, right? It wasn't until she came back with three large female friends that I became aware I had a problem. The largest of them leaned over the sneeze guard, seriously encroaching on my personal space.

"Is your name Tom?" she demanded.

"No," I squeaked, manfully.

"Are you sure?" she asked, taken aback. She looked confused, like when a dog licks ice for the first time. Then she turned positively fierce, and snarled, "A guy named Tom got my friend here pregnant!" She put her fists on her hips and seemed to be challenging me to answer for this crime. The other two moved up to flank her, and the blonde cowered behind all three of them, peeking out at me furtively.

I was at a loss for words. That was not a familiar sensation. My brain tried to process all of the things about this scene that didn't make sense. Obviously, I had another doppelganger named Tom to watch out for. I was too naive to think of reasons someone could be pregnant and not be able to recognize the father (though any number of awful scenarios occurs to me now). And since I was a socially isolated (except for this Fry Guy platform) Southern Baptist teenager, I was primed to be more proud of my own purity than to feel awkward about discussing it. I assumed then that everyone else in the school was wallowing in carnal sinfulness, so I didn't even question the premise of a strange, new, pregnant girl being in our school at all.

The shock of not being able to think of something to say kept me from speaking as much as anything else. I visualized my mouth as a logjam in the North Country, with lots of bearded, en-flanneled miniature Tad-loggers stumbling and slipping on the conflicting idea-logs of fear, outrage, and ill-advised amusement that were trying to flume out of my throat.

One thing I knew: a joke at this point could be fatal.

The situation called for dignity and respect, and so I drew myself to my full 5' 2" height and looked the girl straight in the eye. "Do you know what I'd have to have done with your friend for her to be pregnant?" I asked her. She nodded, looking surprised that things had not come to blows yet, clearly having expected me to leap atop the sneeze guard and proclaim my virility as well as my irresponsibility. "Well, I know what I would have to have done, and I have never done that. With anyone. And if I had, I most certainly would have done my best to remember it."

They looked at each other, and at the blonde girl, who reappraised me with a bit more confidence, now, perhaps even sizing up which of my features weren't exactly Tom-like after all. And what had she to fear of a virgin? She shrugged, and left, her friends straggling behind her. The big one turned around one more time, though, and stuck out a finger.

"I better not find out you're really Tom," she said. She never really looked away; she just slipped out backwards, and the last I ever saw of any of them was her menacing index finger, waggling in the doorway.

Cactus High was a big school with nearly a thousand students, and neither this girl nor her friends ever crossed my path again. I just chalked the moment up to the kind of bizarre and random episode one should expect when one looks like everyone else and becomes Fry Guy famous. Maybe that's what all the adults meant when they told us "Be Yourself"?

Doppelgangers aside, I tried to be myself, even if I looked like everyone, felt like no one, and smelled like French fries from noon until bedtime every day. There are worse ways to smell… and worse things to be, in this world. I was still changing into whatever kind of man I was going to be, and in a couple of years, I would transform again—but at least I wasn't the clueless and lonely kid who had convinced himself he was an alien any more. At least I could stand up and own who I was without antagonizing everyone around me. I would have to live down publicly announcing my virginity, but that was a minor thing to me, and not really a surprise to anyone else.

I'm still glad I'm not Tom.

9

The Horrors, the Horrors

Our hands were clasped, and we gazed deeply into each others' eyes. We had run out of breath, our hearts were thudding with the passion of the moment. We heard music, and we were compelled at that moment to kiss.

We were barely sixteen, and a kiss like that seemed like it would last forever. But it didn't. We heard the crash of a door slamming open behind us, and we whirled around to face the one who had discovered us...

*

On the twenty-third day of the month of September, in a later year of a decade not too long before our own, a young man was chosen to be the heroic lead in his high school's musical production of *Little Shop of Horrors*. In case you aren't familiar with this show, the "heroic lead" is not exactly heroic; he's more of a poorly dressed, awkward loser named Seymour. And I was typecast in the role.

I'm not complaining; after all these years, I still love the part. I can still sing it, and could probably remember much of the dialogue. Performing was a blast and I loved it. The whole cast did: Rick as the sadistic dentist; Keith channeling Levi Stubbs as the voice of the man-eating plant; Paxton as Mr. Mushnik. Stacie, Julie, and Jessica as the Brooklyn Greek chorus. And don't forget the band, tighter than any metaphor I could appropriately use in a high school setting.

But you may have noticed I didn't mention my female lead, yet. And that is because my girlfriend's best friend was cast in the role of Audrey. Which means I should probably update you about my high school romantic life.

If you recall an earlier tale entitled "The Monkee," you will have a good idea of what my love life was like during freshman year. Sophomore year looked to be a little better, as one of my Choir mates seemed to take an interest in me. As thick-headed as I was, Rory eventually convinced me that I felt the same way about her, and we began an awkward, but very sweet, young relationship.

Along with this new girlfriend came something I had never had before: for the first time I had a circle of social acquaintances. Suddenly, I was spending time outside of school with people my own age... and I liked it. But I came to notice that I wasn't nearly as into the relationship as Rory was, and this presented a problem, since all of my newfound friends were actually *her* friends.

What to do? I did what any socially awkward boy in my situation would probably do: I acted like a jerk. But this didn't seem to work. All it did was bring out the "concerned friend" in everyone around me, cautioning me that I wouldn't want to lose Her—the One Good Thing In My Life.

And then came the play. Being cast opposite Audrey was no big deal to me, at first. I hadn't really read the play that closely. So, imagine my utter shock when I learned that we would have to kiss at the end of our big duet, "Suddenly Seymour."

"You mean, we have to like, lean real close and just pretend, right?" I asked.

"No," said our no-nonsense director, "you are going to put your lips together and kiss for the last two measures of the song."

Everybody indulged in an "aw, cute" moment as Audrey and I glanced at each other in horror. Everybody thought they knew why we were so floored, but I don't think they realized that the real problem was that I had not yet kissed my own girlfriend. Yeah, yeah, sweet sixteen and all that... I had a horrible choice to make. I had to move my relationship with Rory (which I didn't really want to be in) to a new level of intimacy that I didn't want to move to, or get my first kiss on a stage in front of who-knew-how-many people.

Audrey was not enjoying the situation too much either. You couldn't even call us a proper love triangle; I don't think we would even make a polygon. Our director kept threatening to short-circuit the issue by having us kiss in rehearsal, but we found a ways to avoid that. Our conspiracy of procrastination wouldn't last forever, however, so in the end, I either summoned up courage, or I caved in to pressure (depending on how you look at it), and I kissed Rory after school one afternoon before play rehearsal.

It's hard to describe the weeks leading up to the show. My new social status was building, and my budding romance was blooming, and yet underneath it all, I was growing more and more unhappy. I couldn't break up with this girl; after all, she was incredibly sweet, and loved by all. Not only that, but Rory's life seemed to be a scary mess compared to the idyllic boyhood full of Star Wars men and long, solitary bike rides through the desert that I had grown up with. Every time I worked up the nerve to tell Rory that I thought we should end it, something would happen: her mother lost a job, her grandmother died, her alcoholic father came back to live with them... one thing after another for months on end.

My family and my church had taken Rory under their wings, and the deeper into my world she was drawn, the less space there was for me. I couldn't help feeling trapped between a duty to do the right thing for Rory and the knowledge that the longer I avoided the break up, the more awful it was going to be for everyone.

The only real escape for me was the play, where I was part of a team, doing something that we were increasingly proud of.

*

Which brings us to the dress rehearsal.

If you've never been in a theatrical production, you can only imagine the value of doing a real run-through, just to shake out all of the bugs. This is where the mistakes become apparent, and fixes can be made before opening night. For Audrey and me, this was the moment of The Kiss. We had stalled and dodged for weeks, but our director was furious that we hadn't done it yet, and it had come down to this. To compound the pressure, our director had decided to make it an "open dress rehearsal." She wanted as many people as possible to come and watch, to see how we would handle the pressure of an actual performance.

How would you handle a first kiss in front of a jury of your bored peers?

We sang our hearts out, and we built to that final note. Our hands were clasped, and we gazed deeply into each other's eyes. We had run out of breath, our hearts were thudding with the passion of the moment. We heard music, and we were compelled at that moment to kiss.

I learned something in the split second after our lips mashed together in that completely unromantic pressure-cooker moment: Kissing is Awesome. Everything I had been told in my life up to that point had drawn a big red "NO" symbol around sensuality. Everything good or sweet about touching someone else had always been tainted by the soul-damning stigma of Sin and Eternal Damnation. Even kissing Rory had been washed over with a feverish guilt because I couldn't control the passion I felt, I knew where it wanted to lead me, and I knew I had no intention of "doing the right thing" afterward.

But this kiss felt completely different, not just because I was kissing a different person, with different lips and a different taste, but because this situation was free of guilt. My mind allowed me to feel this kiss, because neither of us had wanted it to happen in the first place. That freedom let me savor being close to someone in a way that I hadn't known I could be before. In every way that counts, for two full measures of music, I was Suddenly Seymour.

We were barely sixteen, and a kiss like that seemed like it would last forever. But it didn't. We heard the crash of a door slamming open behind us, and we whirled around to face the one who had discovered us: Mr. Mushnik.

Remember what I said about "bugs" in the production? Here was one: Mr. Mushnik's mustache. Paxton had insisted all along that he could grow a mustache for the production. He stopped shaving, I'll grant you, but after six weeks of rehearsal, he had only the barest whisper of hair fuzzing the vermilion of his lip. And so, come the night of dress rehearsal, Paxton showed up with a false mustache, and a bottle of spirit gum.

The spirit gum worked great through the first act, but after our big number, "Mushnik and Son," perspiration overtook inspiration. What Audrey and I did not know as we stood locked at the lip during those final bars of "Suddenly, Seymour" was that Paxton had gone in search of an alternate solution to the false mustache. Thus, when he crashed through the door, startling our hero and heroine in love's stolen embrace, we whirled to find Paxton standing before us... with a Charlie Brown-style zigzag drawn on his upper lip with brown dry-erase marker.

Audrey was lucky; her part called for her to run offstage in tears, which she apparently found very easy to do. I, on the other hand, had to face Mr. Mushnik and look scared, when what I really wanted to do was drop to the stage and roll around in gales of trouser-soiling laughter.

It gets worse.

Paxton's next bit of dialogue leads to the "ah-ha" moment, where Mr. Mushnik accuses Seymour of doing in the dentist, and he cries, "...I found *this*!" as he pulls the dentist's blood-soaked smock from a nearby trash barrel.

Instead, Paxton cried, "...I found *this*!"... and frowned into the empty trash barrel for a moment before saying, "I must have left it in the other barrel." Then he dashed backstage to find his prop.

And there I stood, onstage, every emotion that my hormone-riddled body could evoke fighting for its chance to surface. The music kept vamping—a four-bar repeat of the "Oh, dear" music—and I started to make stuff up.

I have no idea what I said. Something like, "Oh, dear! Oh, me! What can it be? What kind of evidence could he have on me?" Like Shel Silverstein on Tin Pan Alley. I was actually told by some kids who were there that when they saw the official version of the show later that week, they were disappointed that part wasn't in there again!

But the point is that, like all awkward moments, this one passed. I kept my head, somehow, and managed to survive. The show, the kissing, the inevitable break-up with Rory... it was *all* a kind of dress rehearsal, wasn't it? And the moral of the story, of course, is one that anyone with an ounce of common sense will tell you without going through all of the pain and agony: if you can't grow it yourself, you're better off without a mustache.

10
Calling America

My life as a working man started out in what many would consider menial jobs—first as the Fry Guy at my high school cafeteria, then as a carry-out clerk at a couple of grocery stores. After graduating from high school with a few years' worth of work experience on my resume, I decided to trade in the rewards of life as a bag boy and move up to something a little more white collar.

Acting on a tip from a friend-of-a-friend, I applied at a Phoenix-based market research company and was hired to spend my evenings calling unsuspecting American consumers to find out their valued opinions about the crucial inner workings of our economy. For the princely sum of $6 an hour (more than minimum wage!) I could virtually visit the homes of demographically desirable people in a rolling sweep of America's time zones.

You might think with my predisposition against the telephone that I would have avoided this job the way a Congressman avoids accountability—but as the Congressman would probably tell you, you can brazen your way through anything if the paycheck is tantalizing enough. And I'd had my fill of bagging groceries for cranky old farts and dodging their Buicks in 115-degree heat while retrieving their carts. If I could pull down $30 a night sitting in a cubby and reading off a CRT screen for six hours, I was all about that.

"Good evening, ma'am, this is Tad with The Local Market Research Bureau. To qualify for our survey, how frequently do you purchase jeans? And could you please name as many brands of jeans as you can? Thank you, and if you could, please, on a scale of 1 to 10 with 1 meaning 'least agree' and 10 meaning 'most agree,' please rate the following dozen or so statements. First, 'Jordache jeans make me feel like a real cowboy.' ...Yes, ma'am, that was the question... No, I'll need a number between 1 and 10, please. Great! Now how about the statement, 'Wrangler jeans make me look sexy and fashionable...'"

But keeping a straight face wasn't the hard part. No, I realized straight off that I was in a cutthroat and merciless business when our managers explained during orientation how we would be judged. The Bureau paid good money for the lists of phone numbers they pumped through our system, and they expected us to maintain a high percentage of completed calls. We were closely monitored for our performance— with our jobs on the line at any time.

We all had a nightly quota to fill of actual completed surveys, meaning that the respondent qualified on the demographic questions and then actually finished all of the survey questions. If they didn't qualify— because, for example, they didn't wear jeans, or drink beer, or watch nightly news programs—or if we already had a large enough sample for their age, race, or gender—they didn't count toward our quota.

"Good afternoon, sir! I'm Tad with The Local Market Research Bureau. Before we begin, I need to verify that you consume at least three alcoholic beverages a week... No, I don't need a full count, just more than three? Wow, 90? Okay, well done. And have you been drinking alcohol for at least three years? For seven years... 90 a week for... No, that's just... wow. Great, last one. I need to make sure you are at least 21 years old... Ah, well 21st happy birthday! Yes, you barely made it—great timing, sir!"

Our overall performance was judged by whether we met our quota during our shift, and by our rejection rate. We had to track how many calls we made, and whether they were a "Hangup," a "No," or a "Complete." We were not allowed to hang up on a respondent under any circumstances; if they hung up before completing a survey, that counted as a Hangup, but if they simply wanted to refuse to participate, we were required to get them to say "No" at least twice before ending the call. We were monitored at random, so we never knew until after the end of a call whether there was a supervisor listening in, but if they caught you hanging up or leading the respondent to say, "No," you could be sent home.

"Good evening, sir, this is Tad with The Local Market Research Bureau... Why, yes, it should be about 9:30 there... Since I already woke you, could I get you to answer a few quick questions about... Oh, I'm in Phoenix, sir, but could I possibly ask you... I would appreciate it if you wouldn't use that kind of language sir... If I could just get you to... I'm sure a telephone would never fit *there*, sir."

I tried to figure out what my co-workers did to keep their numbers up, but it was tough. We weren't supposed to stray from the script, and there wasn't really any down-time for chatting between calls. Even if I could have leaned over to ask for pointers, my neighbors were rarely people I could talk to. The middle-aged man with the child-molester mustache and bad comb-over wouldn't make eye contact on his best day; the retired schoolteacher lady had her knitting and an acid tongue for every Hangup; the cute girl my age couldn't decide whether to flirt or sneer at me. The only one who even talked to me was the flamboyant Madonna-themed crossdresser who happened to be the roommate of a friend from school. And while I can appreciate now the rare compliment his motives paid me, at the time I was seriously put off by his not-at-all-subtle intentions.

"Good morning, ma'am! The Local Market Research Bureau calling, my name is Tad. Could I ask you a few questions to see if you qualify for our survey on burgers today? Great!"

The stress was surprisingly difficult to deal with. I found myself dreaming in my sleep about surveys; burgers, beer, jeans, and more. I found myself answering the phone at home, "The Local Market Research Bureau..." And despite all my efforts, I couldn't get the hang of boosting my numbers. Even when I had a good call, I could expect a supervisor to come out on the floor and call me out for some mistake.

"You may want to move your questions along a bit next time, Tad."

"But I got the survey done..."

"It's a 15-minute survey about hamburgers. It took you 45 minutes."

"I couldn't help that. She was passionate about Wendy's buy-one-get-two-free offer."

"I realize that, but these weren't open-ended questions."

"We asked how many burgers she buys in a week. She had to average the weeks when she buys four dozen against the weeks when she subsists off the frozen burgers."

"But you let her ramble on."

"I tried."

"Try harder... or you go home."

In the end, I got tired. I was overwhelmed, and I had other things I wanted to do in the afternoon. My shift started strictly at 3 p.m., and school let out at 2:30, so if there was any traffic to speak of, or if I had to stop for anything (like maybe to use the bathroom? I'm only human!) the doors would be shut and I'd be sent home.

Finally, my supervisor pulled me aside and put it bluntly—I clearly didn't want to be there, and while he didn't want to fire me, it was going to happen if I didn't improve all my numbers: attendance, rejection rate, call time, quota. So I went home and started looking for a new job.

It wasn't even a close call.

11

In October

There was a band in the late 1980s who took their name from a US spy plane, and they put out a spare, black and white album with spare, black and white songs full of dust and spindly trees. The sky I'm looking at is a full color version of the album cover, minus the pale, blurred Irish faces. The only blurred face within miles is mine, thanks in equal parts to heartbreak and seasonal allergies.

I'm getting into a white Datsun hatchback with automatic transmission, which I'm not far from discovering it wasn't meant to have. I'm going off to school for the day, and the music of U2's *Joshua Tree* is pouring from my speakers. I'm trying to sing along—I am, after all, a voice major—but I can't duplicate the delicate pain in Bono's voice. My failure galls me, because I feel so superior to the wistful man singing the words. I am so certain I could write that song myself! The jealousy burns in me, and it will be years before I can deal with the fact that it is jealousy. I will never write a song like that. I will barely manage to sing it without my voice cracking.

But soon I will be running to stand still, and I will understand that song.

After school, I will head to my girlfriend's house. She is still in high school, but now that I am not, our relationship is barely legal. I doubt her parents would tolerate me chasing after their daughter if I hadn't been there almost every day for the last four years. She wasn't my first girlfriend, or my first kiss, but she was my first love. Everyone pretends that we are not lovers. Everyone knows we are.

But this is not the beginning of the relationship, and this is not a casual visit. There has been someone else, and I'm enough of a fool—an honest and honorable one, I think—to tell her. It's not a lurid confession of physical transgression, but at our age, that doesn't matter. It doesn't matter that she herself was only the third female to show me any kind of romantic interest, or that I was completely unprepared to handle it when a fourth came along. It wasn't what I did that needed confessing; it was how long I hesitated before saying no. How do you explain that, when you are too young to understand it yourself?

So we sit in the Arizona room—a screened-in patio area with venomous green AstroTurf and wicker furniture—and she smokes cigarettes in defiance of her parents. Her mother sits stoically on the other side of the glass door, watching Oprah, not watching us and certainly not listening as her father flits about through their kitchen. He occasionally pulls a show tune from the bench of the piano and plays a song—"Stranger in Paradise" or "Lara's Theme"— and then puts it away and heads out to his car to leave.

We don't say much, because we know her sister is listening from her bedroom. She sits behind the window screen quietly, thinking we can't see her, with her stereo playing a bizarre mixture of power ballads and this new kind of gritty metal music coming from Seattle. We don't want to corrupt her.

After stilted conversations about school work and making half-hearted plans for the weekend, we get into my car. I have a predictable selection: Paul Simon's "Graceland," Peter Gabriel's "So" and "Us," Harry Connick, Jr.'s *When Harry Met Sally* soundtrack, and *The Phantom of the Opera*. There may be a leftover from summer, like the B-52s and some Billy Joel, but she's gotten sick of those from driving around with me.

We drive to the new park they built in the canal. It only floods in late August and early September, if it floods at all. It is now October, and everyone feels pretty safe at the playground and on the volleyball court. It is, however, a little chilled, since the sun is blocked early down in the bottom of the canal. People are wearing sweat pants instead of shorts, and the cyclists are wearing thin windbreakers. The usual twenty- to thirty-degree drop in temperature at this time of year has given all of the children runny noses, and they play listlessly on the shiny new monkey bars, swings, slides, and merry-go-rounds.

We sit on the decorative river rocks that line the steep sides of the canal above the bike path. We are just under the bridge, and the traffic roaring by keeps anyone from eavesdropping. As though anyone would want to hear such whining and pleading. She doesn't. She is done listening, and even though she did not say so, we know it is over. I take her back to her house in silence, and drive a circuitous route home.

I end up at the park north of where they're going to build the new freeway. It will circle the whole city, they say. I don't believe it. By the time they finish it, the city will have grown around it like the belly of a middle aged man spilling out of his belt. I've even read articles asking for another loop even further out. You see the pattern, even if you're only a community college music student with no future.

The sun goes down slowly when you sit on top of a mountain. Even a worn and stooped hill like the one I'm on towers over the valley. If I were facing south, I could see all the way to South Mountain, where all of the radio and TV towers are. Facing east, I could see Camelback Mountain, sticking up from where it is pinched between extravagant wealth in Scottsdale and hopeless poverty in Sunnyslope. Driving around that one sorry hill is like driving from *Dallas* to *Sanford & Son* with a commercial break in between.

I am facing west, though. That's the direction I want to go. There is nothing out there, once you get past my house and the city where only the elderly live. Who named this place Youngtown, anyway? I climb up a one tree hill, and my mouth fills with a gust of dusty wind. Only two weeks ago the air would have burned from baking in the harsh sun all day, but now it is slightly damp, and full of spores and pollen. I wipe my eyes and nose, and hurry back to my car.

64

At home I call Chris to see what he's up to. He's bored, and wants to go somewhere—how does west sound tonight? I am ready to agree even before he offers gas money, and I grab some supplies on the way out the door. Supplies are two sodas and a few of Mom's cookies.

We head west from his place, taking Bell Road through Sun City, which is Youngtown with a different mayor. We follow it until it becomes a dirt-lined track, and then a dead end. We turn south until we find another major road. We are blaring Queen through the town of Buckeye, and stopping at the Circle K for more snacks for us and the car. We decide to head for Wickenburg, in the other direction. We've switched to the Pogues, and we spit and curse along with the singer for twenty miles before the tape runs out. In the silence I tell him about her, and what I've done.

"Stop," he says, and I stop. He gets out of the car, in the dark, with the wind whipping across the flat land by the quiet road. He walks back up the road the way we came, and I get out, too. "Stay there," he orders, and I do. The car is off the road on the side, with the lights off, and I walk around it, looking up at the stars through the streaming wind-tears. I find Orion, and the Big Dipper, before I give up on keeping warm in my thin denim jacket and get back in the car.

When he comes back, I have James Taylor's *Greatest Hits* in. We ride in melancholy to Wickenburg, which is dark and empty with the hour and the wind. We feel empty, which could be some kind of hunger, and we turn around again, heading home. I know why he's upset, though he doesn't want to talk about it. He tries, anyway. He can't quite bring himself to compare my high school romance to his own parents, or to all the broken or loveless marriages of so many of our friends. We both know it was silly to think two teenagers would go the distance, but that doesn't keep us from feeling let down and hollow. He wishes for the hundredth time that we were old enough to buy, and I agree. It won't be long.

I drop him off, and head back to my parent's house. It is too late, and there are words when I come in. My parents start in cordially—no one wants to offend anyone else. But, they can smell the cigarettes on my clothes, and they can't help talking around their concerns over what I might have been up to. The hints and implications in their words can all mean something else, so there isn't anything I can say to reassure them. The elephant in the room is my future, and all three of us are wondering what I'm going to do, and how I'm going to do it. To them, I'm still the boy in his room with his dreamy imagination. I can't stay a child forever. But I'm not a child. Which is why I should consider... But how can I when... I can feel my eyes glazing over, and I have a vision of squares talking in parallel about circles. They want nothing more for me than the happiness they have. I wanted that, too, but can't tell them how close I came or what I've lost. I laugh. It is misconstrued, and I go off to bed.

I lie staring at the ceiling. The wind is still gusting outside, but tomorrow there will be more of the endless, cold sun. It loses some of its color along with the heat. The cold is only relative, but I think I can feel it, even though I've never lived through what some would call a real winter. Forty degrees is cold enough for me, and that's at least two months and twenty degrees away.

Years go by, with or without those you love. After a while, the songs are all that make sense. Their words aren't forgotten, though your own are. All you have left are images and temperatures, smells and sounds. They mingle with the memories, and the soundtracks take over the dialogue until you almost forget who did what to whom.

No matter how cold Arizona gets, there is always sunshine, and the option to stay inside and pretend that it's warm. But pretending only takes you as far as an old Datsun on a night in October.

12
How Did *That* Happen?

My girlfriend completed a rather drawn-out breaking up process. After that day in October, we had continued some kind of relationship for a few more months, but things had not gotten any better between us. She finally had enough, and told me we were over. I drove to Tucson to talk her out of it, but I failed; and when my Datsun's transmission also failed on the way home from Tucson, I couldn't afford to tow it or repair it. This left me without transportation, which led to the loss of my great job; and since my roommate had flown back to South Africa for the summer, I couldn't make the rent and I lost my apartment.

I moved back into my parents' house, which seemed to have shrunk a bit in the nine months since I had moved out. And, most limiting of all, walking the five miles to work (I had outgrown my bicycle) at Wards department store in the mall was the best prospect I had going.

Time dragged on and things steadily drifted downward over the course of that summer. I alienated my best friend in a misguided attempt to pair him with a girl he liked: misguided because she turned out to like me, and because I was foolish enough to miss all the signals and trusted Captain Morgan to do the match-making.

My parents anxiously brooded off-stage, hoping I would pull my head out of whatever dark place it was stuck in and grow up. I took small comfort from my two remaining friends—one being a Comfort of the Southern variety, the other of the Philip Morris variety—which I pretended not to have, and my parents pretended not to notice. School started, and for the first time since I was five years old, I wasn't going.

I was almost twenty-two, and out of ideas.

I still had my dignity, though. I mustered what professionalism I had and tried to figure out how I was going to pay for the next semester of school while working in housewares. The job itself wasn't bad. It was a step and a half up from the bottom-feeding drudgery of telemarketing or the series of grocery stores I had been working at for seven of the eight preceding summers.

With a little effort, I was able to deal with people cheerfully day after day. After a while, I became the "problem" guy, which didn't mean that I was the one causing trouble, for a change. Any customer that one of my co-workers couldn't handle would be thrust my way as though I had some imaginary authority. If I may brag a little, I was good at it.

One lady, for example, was a regular problem: she brought in all of the junk mail she had collected every two weeks like clockwork. Because she had a store card, a large portion of that mail was from Wards, and she seemed to think that we were personally stuffing the envelopes and sending them to her as some kind of targeted attack.

She was wheelchair-bound, morbidly obese, and also a victim of throat cancer—which had left her with one of those voice boxes that generates a horrible mockery of human speech. Her husband acted the part of the tall, gaunt, and silent valet who propelled her wherever she wanted to go under a fusillade of unintelligible, computer-generated barks from the voice box. Whoever was at the counter when she arrived was met with his blank, fishy stare and her robotic tirade compounded by the added assault of stacks of unopened fliers, circulars, coupon books, pre-approved applications, and full-color advertisements hurled at the counter top. Invariably, they sent for me, because I could understand her.

One afternoon, while helping two flamboyantly homosexual men in matching ruffled leisure suits select throw pillows for their couch, I heard the bi-weekly attack starting up on Michelle, our newest employee. "Chintz!" I decided, tossing an armful of pillows at the indecisive couple, and whirled to Michelle's rescue, leaving them to argue in lisping Spanish over the relative merits of magenta versus burgundy.

"NGET UZ OVF YERR GODDAMNG NGAILING LISZT!" I heard, followed by the soft thump of mail on Formica. This was just before the dawn of the Internet age, and Wards was trying to avoid their looming bankruptcy with an aggressive campaign to recharge their catalog sales. There was little to nothing that anyone could do to get off the company mailing list once you were on it, and I suspect that the Fosters were representative of an American population that was happy to see the company fold a couple of years later.

"Let me help you, Mrs. Foster," I said smoothly. She wouldn't be happy until I "called corporate" and set them straight. I dialed Gary, the owner of the tobacco shop next door, and told him in no uncertain terms that if he didn't remove Mrs. Foster from our mailing list, I would testify in court that he wore women's undergarments and abused zoo animals. Or something like that. Mr. Foster nodded solemnly and eyed a pile of toaster ovens.

Meanwhile, a man had wandered over from the lighting department with a set of almost-matching lampshades. I tried to ignore the brewing storm as Michelle began to argue with him about the price that came up on the register. I had my hands full appeasing Mrs. Foster

"You got the Robot Queen over there?" Gary was asking on the phone.

"Yes, sir," I replied in my sternest tone, "and if you don't stop sending them our fliers, we will lose their business forever!" (They had never bought a single thing from us that I was aware of.)

"Hee hee, thanks for the warning!" Gary said. "I'll take my break before they get here! Even I don't feel right selling her all those cigarettes!"

"But the sign says 20 percent off, and it's sitting there with these shades," the other man insisted to Michelle.

"Well, it's ringing up at $10 each, that must be the sale price," Michelle said. She was casting me anguished looks, begging to be bailed out.

I hung up the phone, and turned back to the Fosters. "If you get any more mail from them, you let *me* know," I told them, and sympathetically dumped their letters into the trash bin. They rolled away, satisfied... until the next mail delivery.

"Help me get rid of this guy," Michelle whispered at me behind her hand.

"Why don't you just give him the discount?" I asked. "It's only two bucks."

She paled at the suggestion. "Not on *my* account! Won't they fire me for that?"

Not wanting to argue in front of him, I turned to the man with the lampshades. "Where was the sign, sir?" He showed me; it wasn't supposed to be there. It wasn't even one of our signs; some joker had brought it over from another store. This guy didn't care about that, though. He by-God wanted those lampshades, and he by-God wanted a deal! I just wanted him to go away.

So, I logged in on a register, rang him up—with the discount— and took his money. "You have a nice day, sir," I said, as sincerely as I ever say it. Just between us, whenever I say the word "sir," it has a special meaning in my mind; an acronym consisting of "suck it" or "stuff it" (depending on my mood) combined with "rambo" or (when I was younger and less sensitive) "retard."

Unless, of course, I respect you.

The man smiled, and cocked his head to one side. "You know," he said, "that showed a great deal of professionalism and leadership. Have you ever considered a career in the military?" I demurred, without laughing. He handed me a business card. "I'm an Air Force recruiter at the processing station in downtown Phoenix. Give me a call sometime, and we can talk about getting you out of retail." I politely tucked the card into my breast pocket.

Dad picked me up from work that night and asked how my day went. I was dying for a cigarette but didn't want him to know I had ever so much as seen one lit. I reflexively brushed the breast pocket of my shirt, where my smokes had formerly resided, and remembered the card.

"I was offered a job in the Air Force," I said, laughing.

Dad didn't laugh.

13
Saying Goodbye

My recruiter told me to stay out of trouble. I was shipping out to basic training in two weeks and all of the paperwork was done; if I got so much as a speeding ticket, it would screw everything up. I figured I was a pretty easygoing fellow: staying out of trouble should be easy, right?

Since I had a plan again, and had a few weeks of pay to play with, I tried to have some last minute fun, so I went to some concerts with my friends. Saw Elvis Costello with the Crash Test Dummies, Huey Lewis and the News, and even Kenny Loggins (thanks to the State Fair). Believe it or not, that was great. Chris decided to forgive me for the incident with the girl and the Captain Morgan, and he came up with tickets to see *Jesus Christ Superstar*.

Chris and I had known each other since at least seventh grade when we sat next to each other in Band. In all that time, he never expressed any desire to learn to drive or to saddle himself with the expense and bother of owning a car. Until now. We were going to travel across town to Gammage Auditorium to see *Jesus Christ Superstar* in his brand new—to him—1978 Honda Civic. He had dubbed it "The Beast."

From my parents' house in the extreme northwest of Phoenix, to Arizona State University in Tempe located to the southeast of Phoenix, meant a journey of about 40 miles in The Beast. We made it there, parked, and waded through the picket line. Four nuns were marching with signs that said "Don't Make Fun of My Lord" or "The Savior Isn't Silly" in front of the theater. A couple of fundamentalist types stood off to one side smoldering at the Catholics for trumping their own demonstration. They made me nervous, and I planned to head for exits on the other side of the theater if they started rioting.

The show was great, though it went a little campy during Herod's big scene. The scene was the one that protesters objected to, of course. Herod danced around in a leather S&M suit, smacking his butt and taunting Jesus, who stood stoically at center stage. I leaned over to Chris and pointed out that Herod's mockery of Jesus is recorded in the Bible, but you never see anyone protest at the book stores. On our way out, we wondered whether the picketing nuns might have appreciated this point... but this conversation died a quick death when we got to The Beast.

The Beast had developed a problem while we were inside enjoying ourselves: three flat tires. One of them was the spare. After a bit of head scratching, and briefly wondering whether the nuns had slashed our tires (we determined that this was unlikely), we decided to limp the aged monster across the street to a filling station and try to inflate them for the ride home. Our plan was to see how far we could get before they went flat again, thinking we could leapfrog across town from air pump to air pump. The only danger there was in running out of quarters.

Alas, after filling the tires up, they were flat again after half a block. We debated turning around to go back to the filling station when I recognized the neighborhood we were in, and suggested that we stop at Emlyn's place. Emlyn was my former roommate. He had returned from his summer in South Africa to attend ASU, and set himself up in a modest one-bedroom place not far from the campus. We invaded his house and tried to phone Chris's dad to come and rescue us. No answer.

"It's alright," said Emlyn. "I'm borrowing a car for the summer. I'll just run you back to Glendale, and you can come pick up The Beast tomorrow." Brilliant!

So we piled into a wee, two-door contraption belonging to one of Emlyn's classmates, an exchange student from Bangladesh, who had left the car but no insurance or registration documents.

"Well," I said, "just don't get pulled over, because I can't afford any trouble this close to shipping out."

73

Chris was dejected. His "new" car was a bust, and he was fuming over the possible costs of getting it repaired, towed, and otherwise relocated back to our side of town. As he fumed, he smoked Camel after Camel, flicking the ashes carelessly out the sunroof. Most of them made it out of the car, but I had to duck a few stray cinders that blew back into the microscopic back seat, where I had folded myself up like a very heavy map.

We were cruising down the road, laughing at our own absurdity, when I began to choke on smoke. It didn't smell like cigarettes, though. I looked down and saw that it was pouring out from *under* the driver's seat.

Emlyn noticed it at the same time and began furiously changing lanes, trying to get to the side of the road. We careened across eight lanes of traffic, screaming as thickening black smoke poured out the windows. The car finally stopped, and Emlyn and Chris leapt from the car like it was about to explode, leaving me stuck in the back. I frantically reached around looking for the latch that would release me from the charbroiler I was trapped in, and realized that there was no way out. This was one of those tiny, late-1980s import cars that seemed roomy enough as long as you weren't a fully grown American wedged in the back seat. I heard yelling from outside the car and heard Chris fumbling around, trying to rescue me. I tried to wriggle my way into the front seat, but I slipped and landed head first on the floor of the car, pinning my hips between the bench of the back seat and losing all leverage. The floor was littered with papers, and I came eye to flame with the smoldering upholstery where the cigarette had fallen.

Then I saw salvation: a water bottle!

I unscrewed the cap and tried to dump the contents on the glowing edges of the carpet but couldn't fit the bottle under the seat. I tried pouring the water into my hand, but there just wasn't enough room for maneuverability. Somehow, though, I managed to soak some of the papers and stifle the flames. The thick, melted-plastic reek began to clear, and Chris finally managed to work the latch and hauled me out by the ankles into the relatively fresh air along the side of the highway.

We sat on the curb staring glumly at the car for a long time, making sure the smoke didn't start up again and watching for emergency vehicles. Four cops passed us and didn't notice three smoke-streaked college-age guys sitting there on the side of the highway.

Then, since these tragedies happen in threes, Chris asked, "Where are my keys?"

After a brief search of the car, he looked down at the road... and saw there, eight feet down in the only sewer grate for ten miles, the glint of metal from his keys. There was nothing that could be done but pile back into our illegal firetrap and make our way north. (Good thing Emlyn hadn't dropped *his* keys!)

By the time we got to Chris's place, we were dirty and desperate. Emlyn had an early class and headed back to Tempe. We only wanted a drink and a soft couch to collapse into. My plan was to crash there and call my folks for a ride in the morning.

Except that we couldn't get into the house. Chris's parents were gone, the house was dark, and not one car sat in the driveway. We just looked at each other for a long minute. Both of us were thinking the same thing: this will be funny in a few years.

Fortunately, we didn't get caught breaking into his house, since I was supposed to be staying out of trouble.

14
Fishing With Dad

I love my dad. Even better, I know my dad loves me. The only trouble is that we are very much alike.

Oh, sure, growing up I used to hear some of the small town chatter that people of my grandparents' generation still believed about fathers and sons. Talk of the way Dr. Eismann's boy acted just like his old man, right down to the way we would tucked his leg up and sit on his own foot when he spoke to people. The whole "he has his eyes and her nose" game they play with newborn babies. I always blew that stuff off until much later, when I saw my own sons turning into me. Then I began to look at my dad in a whole new way.

I mentioned to him how I had noticed that I was beginning to turn into him, and he blanched in horror. "I'm so sorry," he said. We laughed about it too, but there was no denying that sense of dread that men of our line were inescapably cursed to be... well, to be like us. Easy-going, funny, amiable, and yet hapless. A little accident-prone. Somewhat likely to say the wrong thing in public when we get nervous. Nothing flamboyantly evil or wrong, but just us. Frustratingly and unavoidably passing along some kind of dork gene.

My grandfather had a history of clumsiness. He used to restore Volkswagen Beetles—the old kind that came to life in movies—and no matter how careful he was, he always picked up some new and unlikely injury. The trunk lid would fall on his arm when he reached for a tool. A fender would leap off the car and crush his toe. Once a tire exploded while he filled it with air. One car was particularly creative, leaving his arms all scabbed up like a nine-year-old skateboard novice: he named it Fang and painted it a horrible shade of orange out of spite.

Dad's luck was more subtly bad, and of a more self-inflicted nature. On long car trips when we made a rest stop, he accidentally locked the keys in the car. At church picnics, if he was asked to carry any food into the church, he slipped and dropped whatever dish or pie he held top-down on the floor. (He quickly learned to only carry unbreakable things with sealed lids.) I recall one occasion, when after locking the keys in the car while picking my sister and me up at school, we had to cross a busy road to get to my mom and her spare set of keys. Halfway across, while cautioning us to be careful and not to run, his shoes slipped on the hot tarmac. As he went down, flat on his back, he shoved us up onto the curb with his last bit of balance. That was my dad: hapless, but always heroic.

I think it was his awareness of this family curse that made him so careful. He always had a number of projects going on: house repair, car repair, painting, mending, landscaping. He focused hard on each project and didn't like it when I came around distracting him. It's not that he didn't want me around; he was just too used to doing these things alone by the time I was old enough to take an interest in them. For my part, I was perfectly content to wander about in my little fantasy world, playing *Star Wars* or *Indiana Jones* by myself. Whenever I got too close to what he was working on, he would gently mention something else I could be doing.

After he had finished the project at hand, he always came to find me to play ball or go swimming. I think now that he must have felt bad for excluding me, though I didn't take it that way. I never felt neglected at all. Even if I had, I really couldn't blame him. I inherited these features myself.

I am the kid that was playing on the frame of his pickup truck while he tied down a full load of lumber the summer he built our cabin in Colorado. Just as he cinched the last knot around the last bundle of two-by-fours, there was the soft but definite POP *hiissssssss...* of me stepping on the valve stem of his right rear tire. I am also the kid who threw a softball to him while he wasn't looking and popped him in the nose—this happened on the same day that his bandages came off from the surgery on his doubly deviated septum.

I think it was my unique blend of the Callin clumsiness with 1990s slackerhood that led him to seize that chance to prod me into the military. Of all of the slackers in my generation, it was I who'd shown a special talent for apathy, and my shoulder muscles were overdeveloped from all of the shrugging I had done.

"What are you going to major in?" Shrug. "What school will you go to?" Shrug. "How are you going to pay for it?" Shrug. "What kind of job are you going to get?" Shrug. Dad didn't exactly call the recruiter and tell them to come and get me, but after I signed the papers, he acted like he had.

His guilt was palpable. You might have expected him to be congratulating himself for nudging me out of the nest, but he seemed to have some left-over pacifism from the 1960s in his system. I tried to reassure him, telling him that if I hadn't thought it was a good idea I wouldn't have signed up. We weren't at war at the time, and despite the prevailing family trait, he and Grandpa had both survived the Army, hadn't they? Besides, I was going into one of the more cerebral desk jobs in the Air Force. (As we were to find out later, there was no way they were ever going to let me so much as look at a weapon.)

He still felt a pang every time we talked about my pending departure, though. I had a whole long month before I was to ship out, and while I got more and more excited about the big day, he seemed more and more concerned. Until one afternoon, when he came to me with a twinkle in his eye that said he had something special planned, and he invited me to go fishing.

I knew he had bought a boat. I had seen it under the tarp in the back yard. But I hadn't known that it was ready to use, though most of his projects of late had been related to boat repair. He wanted one last father-son event before I left, and that motivated him to finish it up. So I agreed wholeheartedly.

We dragged ourselves out of bed at 3:30 the next morning and packed a cooler full of sandwiches, sodas, and snacks. He waved me off while he hitched up the trailer, so I dozed in the cab of the truck until we were ready. It was a 45-minute ride to the lake. There were half a dozen other boats ahead of us at the little concrete launch slip. When our turn came, dawn was creeping over the circle of low hills around the lake. The lake was still steely gray and in shadow, while the hills erupted with gold rods of light. Half an hour more, and the dome overhead would already be a pale blue, and the lake would already have overflowed with glare and would have started casting shards of it back at the sun. It would have been nice to see.

However, being who we were, this wasn't meant to be. Our turn came and I stood by the water, guiding Dad as he backed the trailer down into the lake. He set the brake, came back, and we shoved off. I held the rope as he went and parked, pulling the boat along the little rocky shore so someone else could launch. Dad came down and we hopped in. The water was lower than either of us had ever seen it, what with the drought being in its fourth year. Dad wanted to row out a good distance before firing up the motor. We got out about 100 yards, almost halfway to the line of buoys marking the edge of the lake proper. Dad dropped the engine down and fired it up.

Vrrrr-RRROOOMMMMM!!! *Clank.*

The clank was a small sound, like a rock off a windshield. He almost tried to start the motor again, but thought better of it. When he pulled the engine back up, the propeller was already ruined. It looked like a rose; all of the propeller blades were folded up and in on each other like petals. Dad looked down into the water and saw a large, concrete block in the settling murk. He uttered the worst profanity I ever heard him use: "Crap." Then his jaw set, and he unshipped the oars.

Yeah, it was funny later. We chuckled wryly over it seven years later, in fact, after I had served my time and returned home with a growing family. He was standing on a chair, helping me put up a shelf in the laundry room. The baby gate was up across the hallway to keep my youngest son from getting into the nails.

"I better watch it. I'm getting to be as bad as your grandfather, clumsy-wise," he said.

Just then, he whacked his thumb with the hammer. Startled, I leapt forward to catch him, and only managed to upset the box of nails. Dad shook his head as they scattered everywhere.

"Well," he said, shaking his head good-naturedly and nursing his thumb, "there's still hope for the boys." The older boy chose that moment to charge around the corner and run headlong into the gate, which gave out. After a full forward flip, he landed on his back, blinking up at the ceiling and gripping the gate which lay on his chest.

We sat there, not wanting to laugh, and watched each other's pained, embarrassed, or dazed expressions alternate on our strikingly similar faces. Three generations of hapless men, slowly turning into each other.

"That's okay," said Dad, "There's still one more boy."

Part II:
Enlistment

Not Everyone Can Be an Astronaut

1

Six Little Words: Basic Training Part 1

You are on a bus. It is the middle of the night. You have been awake for twenty hours, and as the bus pulls through a gate guarded by men with machine guns and faces hidden by the shadows from their strangely shaped caps, you see a bizarre line of buildings that appear to have been built upside down. Their ground floor is half the area of the three upper floors, making them look like a layer cake dropped on its top—a cake made of pale brick with pill-box windows placed high up on the walls. Spotlighting from the ground gives them all an eerie, alien illumination. This will be your home for two months.

The bus pulls up in front of a modular trailer, and you are shuffled off along with the other riders. You have an envelope with six names on it. It holds your paperwork and the paperwork of five other people. The others gather loosely around you; strangers who have been told to stay with you because you hold their identities. You are all herded into lines, which slowly file into the short, narrow building full of uniformed men with bulldog faces, bristly haircuts, and a walk that speaks of violence. They don't look at your faces, and if you make eye contact, they will react as if you have physically challenged them. They constantly shout or sneer because you have failed to do something expected of you, or you have done something wrong.

You are, in fact, incapable of doing anything right. You stand wrong, you sit wrong, you get up when you are supposed to sit—and don't even think about leaning against a wall or on a table. You try a sheepish grin, hoping for someone to say, "It's alright... just do this."

Instead, the person at the desk—holy cats, is that supposed to be a woman?—bellows at you: "Are you *laughing* at me? Get your meat handlers off my desk!"

After another eternity of hurried waiting—going on hour twenty-two—you are herded once again outside. You move in an amorphous mob, a flock of sheep with scuffed sneakers and slept-on hair, while sheepdogs in camouflage and Smokey the Bear hats nip at your heels. "Keep moving!" "Hurry *up*!" "That way, that way, that way! Did your mother have any children that lived?" Their voices are ice, and their words are chipped stone. Hard, cold edges welcome you to your new life.

They are ushering your group toward the upside-down buildings, cutting out smaller groups and lining them up on the asphalt pads under the overhanging ceilings. Someone barks a number, and it matches the number printed on a card in your hand, so you follow the barking and line up with 49 other dazed sheep in jeans and various T-shirts. Now they start the games.

"Pick up your bags! *No*! Not fast enough! Put 'em down! Now, all at the *same time*... Pick 'em up... NO!"

"Stand at attention! Do you know *how* to stand at attention? YOU CALL ME SIR! Everything you say will begin with Sir! Sir, yes, SIR! Sir, no, SIR!"

"What does your shirt say? *Shut up*! I can read! 'Co-ed Naked Firefighter; Find 'Em Hot and Leave 'Em Wet?' What is *that* supposed to mean?"

Three of these shouting men gather around the guy with the co-ed naked shirt. They pepper him with questions, and you stare straight ahead, thanking any god up at this hour that you wore a plain, solid blue shirt today. Yesterday. Whatever. The other guy is flustered, which is the point of this exercise, but he keeps his bearing. He stays at attention, and doesn't look any of them in the eye; they hate that. They hate that they aren't breaking him, so they keep at him, asking him what his shirt *means*. When he finally claims not to know what his shirt means, they sense the weakness. Why did he wear it? He is slow to answer, and they harangue him.

"Why would you wear a shirt when you don't know what it means? Are you dumb? Can't you read it? Why would you buy a shirt you can't read? Why would anyone buy a shirt like that?"

"Peer pressure, *SIR*!"

There is a hanging silence as they all stop yelling, and try to stifle a laugh. He has scored a small point, but one of your fellow newbies fails to hold back a snort, and they are on him like hyenas on a sick zebra. "What are *you* laughing at? Who gave you that haircut? You didn't *pay* for that, did you?"

*

People are surprised when I tell them that I didn't speak for 17 days. Yes, I answered questions, and I called cadence. But I only spoke when spoken to, and gave my reporting statement when required by the Training Instructors: "Sir, Airman Callin reports as ordered." They called that statement the Six Little Words. They made us write it on a slip of paper and repeat it about a thousand times the first morning. For most of us, the boredom was just another test; one of the ongoing mind games, the point being to teach us Self-Discipline and Attention to Detail. But, there were still guys that didn't get it.

"Airman Reams reporting as ordered, Sir!"

"WRONG!! Reams, do it again!"

"Sir," Reams flustered, "Airman Reams reporting as ordered!"

"NO! Are you working for a newspaper? No 'reporting'! Do it again!"

"I don't know what you want!" wailed Reams.

"GODDAMMIT, REAMS! YOU CALL ME SIR!!"

No, I didn't speak for 17 days. No jokes, no asides, no soliloquies. That was how long it took for them to decide to get rid of Reams.

The Six Little Words weren't the only words Reams had trouble with. He was constantly drawing fire for making dumb mistakes, and when they came after him his eyes rolled in his head and he wailed like a whipped dog. He was nervous all the time, always casting paranoid looks at the rest of us. We tried to help him, but he seemed to blame us for watching his disgrace, and he reacted with defensiveness and suspicion. I was reminded of the time I tried to free a dog with a paw caught in a chain-link fence; the dog snapped at me and wouldn't let me near him, while whining that I wouldn't set him loose.

Reams wasn't entirely a victim. They gave him every chance to get with the program. I heard the sergeant pull him aside and talk to him in the Calm Voice. Hearing the voice of an actual human coming from someone in authority almost brought me to tears as he explained to Reams, "We aren't trying to hurt you. We're putting you under stress so you can learn to function as if you were in combat. You need to learn to take orders and do your job no matter what. We have to be sure you won't fold under pressure. You haven't shown me that you get it, yet."

It was nothing we hadn't been told before; they made no effort to conceal the fact that this was one long, grinding mind game.

If you have never served, you may not understand a key element of military culture. Civilians who never had to learn the names of the services are often shocked when they hear the way we talk about each other, and about ourselves. We harsh on each other all the time, and we revel in our stereotypes. We call Marines "jarhead" and "dog face," the Army are "ground pounders" and "cannon fodder," the Navy are "squids" and "seamen"... or did I say "semen"?... and the "Chair Force" is happy if we get called things like "wing nuts" or "zoomie."

It isn't entirely true or fair that the Air Force is known for being Military Lite, but that is our reputation. My uncle Russ was an Army Vietnam vet, and he'd sent me a postcard that read, "Congratulations on joining the USAF. It's a great way to avoid military service!" He sent it knowing that the rule with postcards in Basic Training is that the Training Instructor will read them aloud to the whole flight. But that postcard came later, after what happened to Reams, and after I broke my 17-day streak of not drawing attention to myself.

The point is, Air Force training was different from the other services, and for a reason. Marines have to be tough, so they constantly run. The Army has to be combat ready, so they yell "hoo-ah" a lot. Navy guys have to deal with ship life, so they are taught to swim. We in the Air Force were mostly headed for behind the lines duty; administrative support, medical, intelligence, etc. Even the flight line is well back from the front in modern warfare. The Training Instructors wanted to pick at us, needle us, erode our patience, just so they could be sure we weren't going to go nuts someday and kill everyone in our office over some small thing.

We had it better than the other branches of service, and we knew it; but we all needed some basic training in dealing with authority and working under pressure, and that was what they were giving us. (Not to mention some valuable lessons in hygiene and living among other people, which some needed more than others!) Everyone seemed to understand that. Except for Reams.

But he refused to understand what he was supposed to do. He wouldn't talk to anyone except to complain. He wouldn't do his details, never made his bed right, always left something unlocked or unsecured. If we pointed out a mistake he would grow sly, sneer at us and accuse us of picking on him; if we let him get caught making a mistake, he would cry—literally, with real tears—that we weren't watching out for him. The final straw came the day we went to the medical center for blood testing.

Our flight was fifth in line that day, standing in formation in front of the building in the hot, San Antonio sunshine. The medical center was across the street from the shoppette, where we had been allowed to go our first week to buy essentials: toothpaste, razors, and small uniform items. Reams kept glancing over at the vending machines and payphones, muttering under his breath. Finally, when all of the instructors had their backs turned at the same time, he made his move.

"I've gotta call my mom," he said, and set out straight for the little building across the street. Two hundred and fifty silent airmen stood at attention, no one quite sure what to do. We couldn't stop him without getting into trouble ourselves, and no one wanted to be the one to rat him out. But someone finally uttered a timid, "Sir?" A familiar bulldog face turned back toward us, annoyed... and spotted the tall, gangling form of Reams as he disappeared into the shoppette.

We expected quite a show: shouting, running, perhaps even some physical violence. Instead, our sergeant quietly asked one of the other instructors to keep an eye on us, and left. We filed through the building, gave up our blood, and marched home, where we went straight to our day room and sat quietly on the floor, waiting.

For us, the worst thing that could be done to us, among all of the punishments at our Training Instructor's disposal, was Recycling. To be Recycled was to be taken out of your flight and put back with a newer one—people who were two weeks behind yours, and thus, two weeks further from graduating from Basic Military Training. Recycling was considered the ultimate horrible fate. We had received two Recycles from older flights ourselves, and they were pathetic, broken little men. They were obviously simple, terrified, and dismal at their duties. But they had tried harder than Reams had, and we had done our best to make them welcome.

We couldn't imagine anything worse than Recycling, except, perversely, being kicked out. There had been rumors about those few who had disappeared after only one or two nights. Utter losers who hadn't been able to handle even Air Force basic training, and had quietly gone to the commander and asked to be released. Prevailing opinion (and there were plenty of opinions—just because I didn't speak didn't mean I wasn't listening) was that they shouldn't have signed up if they couldn't go the distance; this was a game for adults, not little children who changed their minds and ran home to mommy! The only thing left for that kind of loser—and this opinion was expressed by everyone up to and including the squadron commander—was a job in a paper hat, serving fried food to people for the rest of said loser's miserable life. Even Recycling was better than that.

After an hour of intense silence, broken by uncomfortable whispers, we heard the door guard let someone in. We heard the taps of our Training Instructor's boots as he strode down the hall. The TI burst into the room, a look on his face that was a mixture of irked annoyance and minor triumph. "Well, flight, Airman Reams will not be joining us for chow tonight. He has decided that learning the Six Little Words was just too hard. He will have to learn a different Six Little Words."

We were stunned. We felt partially responsible, maybe out of a sense of duty to a comrade at arms; maybe just because we couldn't save him. We also felt relief that we wouldn't have to put up with his crap any more. I think this relief was what loosened me up. Relief freed my tongue, and after maintaining a low profile with my long silence, I hazarded a guess as to which Six Little Words Reams would have to learn: "Would you like fries with that?"

Forty-nine airmen and one sergeant burst into laughter, and all eyes focused on me. For a brief moment, I basked in the bonhomie and the attention, but my blood ran cold the next moment as the TI leveled his glittering, predatory eyes at mine and said, "A funny guy, huh? I'll have to keep my eye on YOU, now!"

2

Three Strikes: Basic Training Part 2

"Who likes bowling?" asked our Training Instructor, Senior Airman Young.

Today was Monday, the official morning of Day One of Air Force Basic Military Training, and we had been permitted a total of two hours of sleep—just enough to assure that even the most stressed-out insomniac would have dropped from sheer exhaustion—only to rise to the 0400 wake-up call: "Geddupgeddupgeddup! Get UP!" This treatment was calculated to keep our defenses down, and it was especially effective on the heels a Saturday of travel and a Sunday spent in uniform issue and the barber shop.

Which is why so many of us were dumb enough to raise our hands at his question. "Bowling" turned out to refer to latrine duty.

Thus, I began my Air Force career in my underwear and on my knees, scrubbing the latrine with four other 18- to 24-year-old recruits. Heads freshly shaved, and smelling strongly of new uniforms, quivering after almost two days of mental anguish, we scrubbed the drab tiles and scoured toilets until they were as clean as the medical facilities. We went so far as to use Brasso polish on any exposed pipes we could reach, and to fold the torn edges of the toilet paper roll into neat triangles.

And yet, somehow, we still failed miserably. Even after several days, each daily inspection revealed some missed detail: a stray pubic hair stuck in a remote corner of the shower, a gobbet of shaving cream clinging to the underside of the sink, and even a stray turd which had miraculously appeared in one of the urinals after we thought we had finished our cleaning for the day. Who poops in a urinal?

Our latrine squad was a roaring success compared to our House Mouse, however. Senior Airman Young had reviewed our records and learned that Airman Speck and myself were the two most educated airmen in the flight, having both attended some college. Speck had a degree, though, and was made Mouse—a thankless job that added cleaning the Training Instructor's office and scheduling the 24-hour dorm guard watch to his other Basic duties. I don't know where the name of the job came from, though it seemed to be a form of "go-fer," and I don't know what our education had to do with it; but I silently offered a prayer of thanks that I had never finished that music degree. Speck seemed to take to the job, carrying a little notebook around to jot down SrA Young's instructions and requests from other recruits to swap dorm guard shifts with each other.

The dorm guard monitor part of the House Mouse job was what brought him down. Among his other chores, it was his duty to train the rest of us in dorm guard policies and procedures: how to challenge visitors, what to say, whom to allow in, how to operate the door. Everything one needed to know was even printed on a large chart next to the door. If it sounds easy, that's because it was. Only, no one could get it right.

Day Eight: 0330. Airman Taylor was caught dozing at the dorm guard station by SrA Young's boss, technical sergeant Burns. TSgt Burns was a sour, angry man, aptly named because any shred of sympathy for us had long ago been charred out of him. He withered SrA Young with a blistering stream of invective over having incompetent dorm guards.

Day Twelve: 1115. Reams (of course) allowed the squadron superintendent into the building without checking his ID card. SrA Young, furious, warned Speck that the next mistake made by one of his guards would cost him his job as Mouse. Speck redoubled his efforts to train us, begging us to read the procedures in our manual every spare minute. There weren't many spare minutes, as we were also supposed to be learning everything in the manual for our final written exam: Customs and Courtesies, Air Force History, First Aid, Chain of Command, Code of Conduct, Pillars of Service, and more. Speck sidled up to people during free time and whispered cryptically, "Remember, call the dorm to attention for any officers that enter!" or, "Announce 'Female in the dorm!' whenever a female comes in!"

The first of three Command inspections by the major was scheduled for Day Eighteen. SrA Young savaged us at his daily inspection, and drilled us over every tiny mistake. Turning to Speck, he growled, "You better put somebody *competent* on dorm guard!" He was still smarting from the incident with the departed Reams, who had only the day before been forcibly ejected from our little ball game. We milled about, nervously fiddling with our gear and trying to catch any last-minute errors before the major arrived. That was when we heard Airman Morgan start the door routine.

"Sir! Please present identification!" A brief pause, and then: "Dorm: Tench HUT!" (Barely three weeks in, and we were already barking "attention" as if we were R. Lee Ermey in *Full Metal Jacket*.)

Fifty airmen snapped to attention, and the major came striding in with his executive officer and TSgt Burns. They checked the latrines first (mercifully turd-free) and began working through the bunk and wall lockers in the east bay. All went well, until...

"Sir! Please present identification!" A brief pause, and then, "Dorm: Tench HUT!"

SrA Young's face purpled as he watched the major snap to. You don't call the commander to attention, unless... Into the dorm came the group and wing commanders! The colonel greeted the major and introduced the general, who was conducting a surprise visit and had asked to see one of the inspections. The major sent his XO, a jittery 2nd lieutenant, scurrying out to get the general a pad of inspection forms so he could join in. We were petrified, but things still seemed to be under control. Then, once again...

"Sir! Please present identification!" A brief pause, and then, "Dorm: Tench HUT!"

All eyes shifted to the sight of the general standing at attention, and then to SrA Young, who must have expected the President to walk through the door at that point—about the only reason to call a general to attention at all. Instead, the XO came nervously into the room. SrA Young's face went beyond purple, back around the spectrum to red again, and he ran, elbows pumping, down the center of the aisle between the bunks, his scream of rage building as he went: "No-o-o-o-o-o-oo-oo-ooo-ooo-oooo-ooOOOOOOOOO!!"

He slammed into the wall next to Morgan and screeched into his face, "TELL ME YOU DID NOT JUST CALL A GENERAL TO ATTENTION FOR A LITTLE STINKING LIEUTENANT!!!"

Morgan, already pale, turned green with horror, and—staying rigidly at attention—called over his shoulder. "General!" he squeaked, "At EASE!"

Thus, the job of House Mouse fell to me. Any hope I had to return to anonymity after shooting my mouth off the day before vanished as SrA Young's face split into a Grinch-like grin. "Oh, it's YOU!" he said. "Let's see if you're witty enough to train your flight to guard the stinking door!"

I hated the job from the start. I was struggling enough with my own duties; every inspection found some new deficiency in sock or underwear folding, and even with the help of my neighbors, element leader, squad leader, and the dorm chief (our student commander) some seemingly impeccable item would draw a demerit every time. Adding the Training Inspector's office only made my situation worse, as I had less time to devote to arranging my underwear according to regulations.

Being responsible for assigning the dorm guard schedule didn't help, either. I quickly wearied of hearing people ask for specific shifts and of keeping track of who had swapped with whom. After being awakened twice on my first night to settle disputes between remorseful swappers, I declared that there would be no more trades. Shift assignments would be final when I posted them on the bulletin board each week. My only consideration was to keep someone sharp on duty when we were likely to get visitors, which could be any time.

I struggled on, failing inspections, irritating my fellow airmen with the schedules I posted, and trying everything I could to get my duffel bag folded correctly. SrA Young seemed sympathetic since I wasn't a discipline problem, and he could see I was trying as hard as I could. I made point of keeping my bearing—which mostly meant keeping my mouth shut—even when threatened with the dreaded Recycling. Strike one was my inability to pass an inspection; I couldn't afford any other problems.

"Hey, Mouse," came a voice from behind me. I had decided to get a jump on cleaning SrA Young's area while my squad waited for their turn in the showers, so I wasn't dressed, and I was supposed to be the only one allowed in that room. Startled by the unexpected voice, I whipped around to see Airman Muncie, a skinny kid with a gigantic head that bobbled when he walked. He sneaked into the TI office through its rear door while I was sweeping under the bed. "Mouse, you gotta put me on dorm guard at night."

"I don't do requests," I snapped. I didn't trust him, either. He was supposed to become an SP, the Air Force's Security Police, but he hadn't shown any of the qualities typically associated with cops. For example, at the rifle range, he dropped his M-16 the first time he fired it as though it had turned into a snake, and wailed, "I can't DOOO it!" until they came and took him away.

"C'mon, man," he persisted. "You oughta put me on at night... You need me!"

"Why?"

"'Cause I like to creep," he said, a gleam in his eye.

The thought of this weird little man—like Gollum with glasses—lurking near my bed while I slept gave me the cold shivers, and I kicked him out of the office. Before he left, he hissed an empty threat at me, and slammed the door.

I heard something fall behind the desk and shatter.

I dove under the desk and found the remains of one of SrA Young's prized awards: a model of one of the missiles he had worked on before joining the Training Wing. Before I could decide what to do, the door opened, and there stood SrA Young, looking down on a cowering airman who was sitting on the floor of his office in his underwear, and holding a broken missile.

Strike two.

*

We had all been warned: anyone failing this next inspection would be sent to the superintendent to be considered for Recycle. TSgt Burns had promised that someone would go by the end of the week; we were SrA Young's first solo training flight, and TSgt Burns felt that our lackluster performance would only improve if he followed through on that ultimate of threats.

Three of us failed that inspection. I was one of them. We were told to line up at attention next to the door. TSgt Burns was called on the intercom, and the other two failures began to swoon and moan, tears welling up in their eyes. I was merely angry, and stood locked at attention, gritting my teeth.

On dorm guard was my friend, Jay. I had specially selected him for this shift so that someone I trusted would be on duty during the inspection. He had performed flawlessly... until TSgt Burns' face appeared mashed in the window and demanded to be let in. Jay did well, following the script on the door. Until, that is, TSgt Burns, the sadist, left the script.

"Sir! Please present identification!"

"You just called me! Lemme in, you piece of crap!" bellowed the Evil One.

Rattled, Jay managed to follow the directions on the board by the door, and said, "Please report to the orderly room for assistance, sir."

"I just CAME from there! You know who I am, now let me IN!" TSgt Burns himself had taught us the class on dorm guard procedure... especially stressing the policy against personal recognition. At this point, Jay was supposed to repeat the previous instruction and then call downstairs for help. Instead, he said:

"NO!"

TSgt Burns blinked, and whispered, "What did you say?"

"I said, NO, I can't do that, sir!" Jay shouted. You could safely say that he had lost his cool.

TSgt Burns went berserk, hurling himself against the door, screaming, and snarling like a pit bull after a rabbit in its hole. The thick, steel door shook in its concrete frame. Saliva dripped down the outside of the window. SrA Young strode to the door and let him in.

Crossing the threshold, TSgt Burns transformed into the picture of composure, and turned to Jay. "Who is your dorm guard monitor, airman?" Jay, standing at attention now, pointed at me. Me, against the wall with the other two blubbering on either side of me, an obvious trio of losers. My insides churning, I stood staring fixedly at a point about six inches in front of my face; precisely the space where TSgt Burns placed his face as he said:

"Pack your bags."

Strike three.

3
Deja Vu Again: Basic Training Part 3

Do you ever get *deja vu*?

Perhaps you do when you are standing back outside that strange, alien building again, holding all of your worldly possessions in a duffel bag. Five weeks ago—a swiftly receding eternity ago—you were standing here facing the unknown along with 45 others just as scared and sleep-deprived as you. Now you are facing the prospect of meeting 49 new others who have gotten used to showering, eating, and learning side by side for three weeks. You are going to be the outsider, now. You are the Recycle.

For five weeks you lived under the constant threat, which the leadership was always careful to say was not a punishment. "Recycling an airman is just a way of ensuring that everyone gets the training that they need," is the official explanation. You watched carefully when they brought Recycles into your flight; simple boys with slack jaws and glazed eyes who obviously didn't know ass from elbow or shit from shinola. To be fair, you don't know what shinola is, either, but you're pretty confident you could pick it out of that line-up.

Of course, you also thought you could learn to fold your underwear well enough to pass an inspection.

Do you ever get *deja vu*?

Perhaps you do when you are staring up the stairwell at the door to your new flight, and the only difference you see between it and your old one is the number on the wall. Five weeks ago, you were pretty sure the worst year of your life was behind you. The hard luck, the cruel woman, the indignity of returning to your parents' house and realizing that you were pretty much to blame for the whole mess was giving way to a new life. And in five short weeks you have burrowed your way back to rock bottom.

You choke back a hysterical giggle as the dorm guard crisply and efficiently goes through the entry routine—the same routine you watched your old flight botch time after time, sending you here as a result. Well, to be fair, it was that and the underwear. Then you are inside, being greeted by a guy with flinty eyes and the kind of jaw you generally associate with Batman. He is your new dorm chief.

Deja vu never lasts, fortunately, and for you it stopped when you came through this new door.

The dorm chief is the student commander, usually chosen at random from the ranks of each flight. Your old dorm chief was a soft-spoken boy from West Virginia whose name, Mullins, was quickly corrupted into "Muffins" behind his back. He had always seemed a little overwhelmed. This new guy's name is Shocke and he exudes authority. If it weren't for the trainee name tag and the telltale stubble on his head from his "Welcome to basic training" haircut, you would have guessed he was one of the TIs.

You're actually glad it's him greeting you instead of the TI. This flight belongs to SSgt Perro, a tiny woman with a huge presence. You remember hearing her march her flight and you shudder at the thought of that shrill, vicious voice, yelping like a steroidal chihuahua. No one messed with her. One foolish airman—obviously a defensive lineman from some inner city high school—made a snide remark within her hearing during PT. Something about female airmen being allowed to do the pushups "on their knees." There is nothing as chilling as watching a skinny, five-foot woman bringing a six-foot, 210-pound man to tears so quickly.

Shocke seems to be as no-nonsense as SSgt Perro and wastes no time in orienting you to your new environment. "We're going for Honor Flight," he begins. "I don't know what you did to get Recycled, and you don't have to tell anyone, but if you do anything that threatens our chances to win, I'll make sure you disappear again." He manages to say this without sounding confrontational or threatening. "If anyone gives you any trouble, tell your squad leader, or come straight to me and we'll deal with it."

You are shown to your new bunk and given a general introduction. You can't help feeling like a bug under a microscope, even though no one is paying particular attention to you. All you can do is unload your duffel and put your wall locker in order. When you finish, you turn to find the squad leader, Larsen, has been watching you, and you offer a wan smile.

"You seem to know what you're doing," he says. "Do you have any questions, yet?"

You shake your head and start to make up the bed. He helps you get the sheets on, but when you spread out the faded olive-green army blanket—known as the dust cover—he recoils. There are coin-sized white spots all over it, which you assume to be bleach stains.

"Oh, crap!" Larsen squeaks. "Don't use that!" He calls Shocke over and takes away the bedding.

"I'm sorry," Shocke says, briskly. "We were supposed to get you clean linens. The guy that used to be in this bunk got sent to the Med Center for psych evaluation yesterday. The guard caught him...um..." He fumbles for the right word, and blushes a little. "...pleasuring himself." He strides off with the wad of offending linens, and the rest of the group offers apologetic mumbles to you.

Other than that, things go pretty smoothly.

After a day or two of handling your duties competently and staying out of trouble, people start to accept you. You let them believe you were Recycled solely for failing inspections and they offer to pitch in to help you pass the next one. Oddly, you pass with very little help.

Since you already completed all of the mandatory training for week four, you find yourself left alone to guard the dorm while the rest of the flight visits the rifle range and attends classes. You become a minor celebrity with your foreknowledge of the different activities they've heard so many rumors about. You resist winding them up over the number of vaccine injections they'll get (only four), and the supposed violation they all fear from some rumored medical exam (no cavity searches), and tell them all about the obstacle course. Excuse me, the Confidence Course.

You are even accepted to the point that your squad lobbies SSgt Perro to allow you to re-do the Confidence Course with the flight rather than stay in the dorm, much to your relief. Not only were you incredibly bored with that duty, but you were starting to have trouble staying awake—a fate worse than Recycle awaited the sleeping dorm guard.

And no way were you going to ask her yourself.

The next morning, when your new flight enters the chow hall for breakfast, you spot a familiar face working behind the food line. The new flight had just finished a week of Kitchen Patrol before you got there, and now, it is apparently your old flight's turn for KP.

You aren't supposed to talk in line, but you risk a greeting. Your old flight mate whispers a quick hello, and leans forward: "They aren't treating you bad, are they man? 'Cause if they're picking on you at all..."

"No," you say, "They've been great."

And then Shocke is there. "Is there a problem?" You tell him who the KP guys are, and his eyes narrow. "If they're picking on you at all..."

It's touching, actually. Forty-nine people on each side of the line are actually concerned about your welfare. Ninety-eight people ready to jump to your side if you need help. You coast the rest of the day on a cushion of comradery.

There's only one real problem brewing: you are getting sick. You don't let on that you aren't feeling well for fear of being Recycled again. This close to freedom, you aren't about to risk it; there will be time for illness *after* week six. But the long days spent on your feet guarding the empty, overly air-conditioned dorm, alternated with marching in the 104-degree San Antonio heat has conspired with daily exposure to the microbes of 100 strangers to bring you down.

After keeping up for a couple of days, your body has had enough; while standing in line in the chow hall, you collapse.

When you come around again, you're sitting on the floor with your head between your knees. SSgt Perro is asking you questions, and you hear yourself answering from ten miles away. "Are you alright?" Yes, ma'am. "Can you get up?" No, ma'am. "Why didn't you go to sick call?" I didn't want to get Recycled again.

"I respect your tenacity, airman, but you need to take care of yourself!" She is speaking kindly, and she doesn't sound like a mad chihuahua. She sends you to the clinic, where you get a nap and some medication. You feel better in the morning, and the last week cruises by.

So now, you've done it. You made it through Air Force Basic Military Training.

In some ways, you aren't sure what you have learned from it. Attention to Detail? Trust in Authority? Reliance on your Teammates? Maybe it is all just a screening process to keep out the fatally insane and the obvious nut-jobs, like the unmourned Reams. All you know is that you are proud, and that you are excited about moving on to the language school.

And that new, proud feeling is the opposite of *deja vu*.

4

Welcome to the Defense Love Institute

"I am going to give you some advice, which, statistically, forty percent of you will ignore," said the stunningly beautiful airman with the green rope pinned to her left epaulet. "Do *not* get married while you are here."

We were lined up in a parking lot, standing in sunshine and 65-degree weather, and marveling at the beauty of our new surroundings. Our parking lot was located at the back of a compound of three large dormitory buildings. Wooded hills stretched steeply upward at one end and steeply downward on the other. I was actually having some difficulty standing at attention because my brain kept trying to turn the line of the steep hill into a horizon, and I fought the impulse to lean to one side.

I kept my eyes fixed on the airman with the green rope, and tried to process what she was telling us. I just said she was stunningly beautiful, but I really wasn't in any position to judge. I had spent eight of the longest six weeks of my life in the flat, hot San Antonio summer, and now I was standing on a hill in Monterey, California, spending a day following her around on our orientation tour. She could have looked like Newt Gingrich, and she would have been the most beautiful woman I had seen in two months.

"Come on," she said, turning on her heel, "We need to get you up to the shoppette and back before lunch." We followed her to a path leading steeply up the hill.

The Presidio of Monterey has hosted the Defense Language Institute since 1946, just after the end of World War II. Originally a series of forts established by the Spanish in the 18th century, the modern Presidio consisted of a series of Cold War-era buildings which sat perched on the hills overlooking Monterey Bay and the famous Cannery Row that John Steinbeck wrote about.

Our group of new arrivals had flown in over the course of the previous weekend. My own group of three had been packed onto a flight from San Antonio to San Francisco, and from there we had transferred to a small charter aircraft capable of landing at Monterey's small airport. I should have been terrified, bouncing up from the fog-shrouded San Francisco airstrip into the turbulent cloud cover the city is known for, but when we popped out into the brilliant sunshine and saw the Golden Gate and Coit Tower below us swaddled in fluffy cotton wadding as far as the eye could see, fear gave way to wonder.

We landed, were retrieved by the squadron's white van and deposited with our belongings in the A Flight day room—a dorm full of living room furniture and a small television where airmen could spend their free time. My group of three had been joined by others until there were a dozen of us. We were eventually assigned rooms, and now we trudged together around our new habitat.

I couldn't speak for everyone else, but my sense of wonder was still with me as we crested the hill, and I looked back to see the campus and the bay beyond it. I was slated to begin the next Arabic course in a couple of weeks, so I knew that I would have at least 63 weeks to enjoy that view, and I turned back to join the whispered speculation on whether our green rope escort was speaking from experience on the marriage issue.

My roommate was chattering most enthusiastically about her. He was a little guy from Maine who had been in my group of three flying out of San Antonio. His name was Airman First Class (or A1C) Weller, and he had quickly zeroed in on me when room assignments were made on that first day. I was glad he had, as we were two of the older guys coming out of Basic. We had both been through college, and the high school guys still seemed a little immature to our seasoned eyes.

"Even if she's single," Weller was saying, "I don't think she's going to have time for a bunch of newbies." If she could hear us, our escort was wisely ignoring us. She took us into the sprawling building at the top of the hill which served as the Base Exchange. She explained that since we were technically on an Army base, we should refer to it as the "Post Exchange" or PX, but that almost everyone referred to it as the "shoppette" because it was much smaller than what one would find on a full military installation.

Life at DLI would prove to be full of these kinds of nuanced learning experiences. All four branches of the military sent students here to learn a variety of languages for different military missions. One thing we would not learn was what those missions were; that kind of information was a well-guarded secret. But we did receive a crash course in all of the ranks and personality quirks associated with each service branch.

Terminology was an important divider. Air Force people technically lived in *dormitories* while the Army and Marines dwelt in *barracks*, even though our buildings were identical to each other. The Navy and Marines referred to all doors as *bulkheads*, all floors as *decks*, and all restrooms as *the head.* Army and Air Force had *latrines*, by contrast. And when it came to addressing the non-commissioned officers—*sergeants* for everyone but the Navy, who called their sergeants *petty officers*—Navy and Air Force could call anyone who outranked them "sir," while the Army insisted on calling their NCOs either *sergeant, sarge,* or if they thought they were in trouble, by their actual full rank. Marines insisted on using the full rank and last name of everyone they addressed, every time they addressed them. Everyone shortened any common phrase to its initials, of course: "non-commissioned officers" were NCOs, "Defense Language Institute" was DLI. That practice was universal.

The airman with the green rope who was, by this point, bringing us back down the hill with our purchases, was a student leader, so she was there for a language class, like the rest of us, but had volunteered for the extra responsibility. The green rope meant that her job title was "squad leader." All of the USAF students at the time were assigned to the 311th Training Squadron, and the squadron was broken into six flights. Where you lived in the building determined which flight you were in, so the layout of the building was pretty important to us.

Our building had two wings—one for men, one for women—with three floors in each wing. Alpha Flight was the only co-ed flight in the building, because that was where all newcomers were assigned. The first floor of each wing housed Alpha Flight airmen, and the commander and staff had offices in the central rooms in the men's wing. The second and third floors of the women's wing were Bravo and Charlie Flights, and the corresponding floors on the men's wing were Delta and Echo Flights. Married students were authorized to bring their families to Monterey and lived in base housing on Fort Ord, which was eight miles away from the Presidio, on the other side of the town of Seaside; they comprised Foxtrot Flight.

The stairway for each wing was in the center with a bay of rooms on each side: A Bay and B Bay, with the rooms on each side of the hall making up a *squad*. The student leaders, then, were two green ropes, or squad leaders, two to a hallway; above them, there would be a yellow rope, or bay chief, in charge of their two squads; and above the two bay chiefs was a flight commander, or red rope. These seven students on each floor were responsible for assigning daily housekeeping details and performing regular inspections on their flights. We would learn that there were other, less official responsibilities tied to their shoulders along with those ropes.

But at the moment, it was enough for us to settle into our rooms, unpack our belongings, and get uniforms ready for the following day's activities. For Weller, this meant shedding his boots and uniform blouse and trying out his new ironing board. Of course, as soon as he did so, there was a knock on our door.

"We're not supposed to be out of uniform outside our room," he said. "Does that mean I have to dress to open the door?" I shrugged; I was in my bunk, wearing the USAF t-shirt and shorts we would be wearing to our daily physical training (or PT), and reading a new Tom Clancy book.

It wasn't a bad question. Part of our orientation involved a detailed explanation of the Phase Program, which outlined what we were and weren't allowed to do depending on what week of training we were in. We were in Phase One, which meant being in uniform any time we were outside our rooms. Phase One lasted until the end of the first full month of our class, and none of us had started class, yet. Phases Two and Three loosened up restrictions on when and where we could wear civilian clothes, and Phase Four, which was reached after four months, meant that our time was our own outside of school and official squadron activities.

All of these phases also depended on staying out of trouble and keeping our grades up. Being "phased back" was a common punishment for infractions from being caught violating curfew to failing to turn in homework, or for any number of other missteps.

Not being one to take chances, Weller put his blouse back on and laced up his boots before opening the door. Our squad leader was impatiently tapping his pencil on the door and doing a decent rendering of the rhythm from Jimi Hendrix's "Fire."

"No, Airman Weller," he said, "You don't have to dress to answer the door. And you can go to the latrine in your shower shoes and PT gear, if you want. It gets cold, so you might want to get a robe."

We had a lovely chat about rules, exceptions, and our schedule for the next day, which included finally learning our class start dates. "What language are you guys supposed to be?" he asked. Weller said Chinese, and I replied that I had Arabic. "Weird," the squad leader said. "I'm in Chinese, too. I'm not supposed to have any Arabic students in my flight. I guess we'll sort it out tomorrow."

I had a sinking feeling. I had been looking forward to Arabic because I knew most of the bases for Arab linguists were in places I wanted to visit. The only language I did not want was Korean, because my recruiter had warned me that the only two places you could go with that language were stateside and Korea. I didn't have anything against Korea, but it sounded limiting. I told myself not to panic; we would sort it out in the morning.

In the meantime, there was a more pressing concern, as one of the other new guys from down the hall had knocked on our door seeking refuge from his own room.

"Can I hang out with you guys for a little while? I just walked in on Sheldon spanking the monkey, and I don't want to be in there right now."

Weller and I glanced at each other, inwardly adding this to the reasons we were glad we got to choose older, wiser roommates than the others.

*

That limbo time between arriving and starting class was referred to as Casual Status. Being "on casual" meant that after morning formation, our flight commanders would hand out any special assignments for the day, which could be any kind of unskilled labor requested by anyone on the post. Some days, the grounds-keeping staff might ask for some people to mow grass; other days the laundry might need people to handle an incoming shipment of sheets.

There were also more permanent jobs for people who found themselves on casual for more extended periods of time. There was a pregnant airman who had graduated her class but couldn't travel until her baby was born; she was given a job in the security office running paperwork. There were a few people who had washed out of their language programs and were waiting for orders to see what their fate would be. They seemed sad and sullen, and we didn't want to entertain the possibility of becoming like them. Some of these were assigned to shifts working the Charge of Quarters desk, which was responsible for running hourly security inspections after hours and on weekends;

everyone in the squadron took at least one turn at working a mid-watch on CQ during their time at DLI, but casual status left one vulnerable to working night CQ on a more permanent basis.

Since we had our meeting to receive our class assignments, we were just given cleaning details and told to report to the Commander's hallway at 1000. The work went quickly, even dragging it out and cleaning everything twice, and I ended up in the day room at 0930 wishing I had my book or something to do besides listen to everyone gossip. By this point, only a few days in, I felt like I had already heard everything interesting that this group of people had to say.

Ever since I had outgrown my middle school isolation, I felt more at ease making friends, but I was still the outsider in social situations. In the status-obsessed high school environment, I never felt like I had a clique to belong to. I was a Band kid, but that wasn't my identity the way it was for some of the other kids. I did choir and theater, but after peaking with my turn in *Little Shop of Horrors* my sophomore year, I had been less involved in both. I did well academically, but I wasn't up for the challenge of keeping up with the devoted honor's students in their quest for the highest GPA.

Now I was at DLI, surrounded by people who had lived that same experience, and while they all bonded over this, I found the experience of being surrounded by my own kind to be very isolating. I was more concerned about the course of my training and whether I was being bumped from my Arabic class. Weller was excited about the possibility I'd be in Chinese, but it wasn't an option I'd ever considered; at least it wasn't Korean, so I would have more options for my assignments.

At last, the first sergeant came into the room, and barked at us to form up and march down the hall to the conference room. A first sergeant is a special job, usually held by the highest ranking enlisted person in a squadron. The Army and Marines have different traditions for addressing them, but in the Air Force, they are usually referred to as the "First Shirt" or just "The Shirt." They often deal with administrative punishments, and ours was about to give us a rundown about her pet issue in that conference room. Once we were crammed in there, she proceeded to deliver a long lecture on the subject furthest from anyone's mind: marriage.

"This school has the longest classes of any training program in the military," she said. "The shortest language program here is nineteen weeks. That is less than six months, but it is one week shy of counting as a permanent change of station. Many of you have courses which are 47 or 63 weeks long. Once you leave here, however long your language might be, you will proceed to Goodfellow Air Force Base for 19 more weeks of specific job training.

"DLI has the highest marriage rate of any school in the Air Education and Training Command. Goodfellow has the highest divorce rate of any school in the AETC. This is why we have earned the nickname 'Defense Love Institute.' The wing commander keeps trying to figure out how to lower the divorce rate, but I know what your game is. You all get here, fresh from of being isolated from the opposite sex for two months, and think you're safe because you've been tested for every disease known to man, and you go nuts.

"Then you get to the fourth month, and once you're on Phase Four, you get tired of living in the dorms. The idea of getting married and getting a house over on Fort Ord sounds pretty good. We've even seen some students get married, take their three bedroom house, and each take a room, then rent out the third. I need you to understand: we are onto that game! It is illegal, and we will prosecute you if you try it!"

All of this was becoming infuriating to me. I had no intention of marrying anyone, and the first sergeant's speech was only putting ideas in the heads of my companions—a few of them were eyeing each other from across the room, as if assessing their suitability as a roommate.

At long last, though, class assignments were handed out.

"Callin!" barked the first sergeant, "Your Korean class starts Monday. Congratulations."

"But, ma'am—" I began to protest.

"Nope. You get what you get, airman."

And that was that.

5
Chicken Poop for Your Soul

Monday morning, 0643: formation between the wings.

Every Monday morning, on the strip of blacktop between wings of the long, U-shaped barracks, several hundred young airman formed up into straight lines for a quick formality: roll call, announcements, and maybe a little motivation.

0644: A1C Charles Pierce III stood facing half of his flight with a clipboard and an exasperated expression on his face. Formation officially started at 0700 when the entire squadron would be brought to attention for the commander. A1C Pierce had been warned several weeks prior that members of his flight had been spotted showing up late, sneaking into the formation by mingling with the trickle of Army, Navy, and Marine students who flowed by the group on their way to the only entrance to the chow hall.

0645: A1C Pierce had announced two weeks ago that anyone showing up after 0655 would be counted as late, which had not deterred a hard-core group of dissenters from arriving at precisely 0656. He had then announced that the following week—this week—anyone arriving after 0645 would be late... and would be dealt with. He fingered his red rope, a sign of his authority as the flight commander, and checked his watch.

0646: "Tench-HUT!" Pierce cried. Only half of his flight was there, and they shuffled haphazardly to attention. "What is wrong with you people!" he yelped. "I said to be here at 0645 today for attendance."

"Go bend a pipe," someone muttered from the back (it might have been me).

"We *are* here, Chuckles," someone else pointed out. "Take your fuggin' attendance."

"Look, you bastards, I'm the flight commander, and I have the authority to drag you all out here as early as I need to, to make sure you're on time for the commander. Don't make me form you up at 0600 for an 0700 formation, 'cause I'll do it!"

He began to call names and check them off his list as they answered. He was almost finished when he realized that even though he was missing nearly half of his people, he had marked off everyone as present. "Hey, you're not answering for people who aren't here, are you? DAMMIT, I..."

"SQUADRON! Tench-HUT!"

0700: Pierce snapped to and dropped his clipboard. Snickers rippled through the flight, which was now nearly completely present (turns out some of the members had been hiding in the next flight over). And now the commander, Lt. Col. Gallegos came striding out to face to the squadron. When I arrived at the Defense Language Institute, the USAF commander was a very involved and down to earth character who knew and liked the students under his care. Unfortunately for me, in a pattern that would prove to hold true throughout my career, the competent commander was quickly promoted and replaced by someone who thought that being in command was like running a church youth group.

"Good morning, squadron," she warbled happily. "I have a special treat for you today. I know some people have been complaining about the new rules in place. Just remember they are there for your safety. If none of you drinks, smokes, or has sex, then nothing bad can happen to you, am I right? RIGHT!" She beamed out at us, basking in our relief at finally being safe from our vices.

"But I am told that morale is slipping, so I have been reading from the book *Chicken Soup for the Soul*. Let me tell you, it gives you a great outlook on life. Think of your life as if you were in prison, and you begin to value each ray of sunshine that manages to find its way through the bars of your window!"

"Great scott, she's going to put bars on the windows!" someone stage whispered. The commander's eyes narrowed, but she pressed on.

"Just remember the inspiring story of Abraham Lincoln, everyone. He was born in a log cabin that he built with his own hands—" (We flinched collectively as a sailor walking by snorted at this.) "And," she continued, "despite his poverty, he grew up to lead us as President through the most horrific war imaginable. He was constantly depressed, and his wife was insane, and just before he died, he found out his son was taking bribes in his name... but he didn't let that stop him! He would have kept on going, if he hadn't been so tragically killed.

"Now, keep all that in mind today as you go to your classes. Some of you will be taking your final language tests this week, so study hard. Especially you Arabic students! Remember, if little retarded Arab children can learn Arabic, then SO CAN YOU!"

And with that, the squadron was called to attention, the commander marched briskly back to her office, and everyone was released to their flight commanders. Pierce turned around, stooped, and picked up his clipboard.

"So now we're retarded inmates in a prison run by a nut who thinks she's Abraham Lincoln?" someone asked snidely.

"What time you want us next week, Chuck? 0500?"

Pierce looked around at them, fingering his rope. "Just don't be late. 0700."

And with the Army, Navy, and Marines streaming by—and trying not to laugh outright at the speech they had just heard—the airmen scattered to their various cells to look for sunshine.

6

The Jarhead Who Laughed

There is one fundamental Thing About Me that you must understand: I am not comfortable until I have made you to laugh.

It doesn't have to be much. Of course, if I had my way, every bon mot would bring laughter. Every wisecrack would prompt a shared grin. Each pun would be a serve which would lead us through the Volley of the Shadow of Wit. But I will settle for a mercy chuckle, or a groan and an eyeroll; even the grimace recognizing a misfired punchline will make us friends. It is the connection of minds that I crave.

And so when I met Steve, the Marine, I knew I faced a formidable challenge.

Steve was the original Robo-Grunt. He moved with a purpose, or not at all. Every turn he made was a right angle. He sat at attention with his Korean dictionary aligned in the upper right corner of his desk, and his pencils—all freshly sharpened with the points to the right—rested in a row on the left. He was crisp, he was sharp, and he wasted no movement.

I didn't stress about his stoic demeanor at first. I don't need immediate gratification; I don't need constant adoration. Everyone is human, so I waited for my opportunities, and took them as they came.

There were three Marines in that class; the other two were easy prey. Marines are generally smart people, and coming fresh from boot camp, they have egos the size of Chesty Puller's medal rack (that's big, kids). They don't expect much from non-Marines, especially not from slacker airmen like myself. So all I had to do was a little self-parody to knock off the first; referring to myself as a "wingnut" did the trick. The second, a Filipino lad, took a little more effort. I asked him very seriously for the Tagalog word for "penis," and when he told me it was "penis"—Tagalog borrows many English words—I made a big show of writing it down.

"Did I spell that right?" I asked, showing him the name of the insufferable Army private who sat next to him. Two down.

But Steve was tough. He rarely spoke, and when he did, he sounded like he was quoting regs. "What did you have for breakfast, Steve?" Dave might ask. Dave was one of the three Dave Williams in Alpha Company (one of the two real ones, in fact; more on that in a moment), and he happened to be our class section leader. Enlisted Army guys get twitchy about being called "sir," and usually a Marine would have addressed Dave as "Specialist Williams," but because Steve called him "sir," I knew there had to be a wit in there somewhere.

"Sir, eggs scrambled; juice, apple, 8 oz.; toast, qty. 2, no butter," Steve might reply to the breakfast question. Ask him how he slept, he would tell you the time of onset of R.E.M. sleep, and report any incidents such as head-calls. Very perfunct. With such a smooth rock face to climb, I got a little desperate.

Several weeks passed, and much drama had unfolded. As I mentioned, there were two Dave Williams in our class: Specialist Dave Williams, and Private Dave Williams. The way Army rank works, there is also a "Private First Class" rank in between the other two. Our other class leader, Specialist (or SPC) Baron had suffered successive weeks of roommate trouble; his platoon kept sticking new arrivals in his room the day before inspections, and then when he failed his room inspection, the platoon sergeant would blame him for not demonstrating adequate leadership. Then they would find a permanent room for the new person, only to repeat the process the next week.

When SPC Baron's most recent roommate had skipped out, leaving a huge mess for Baron to clean up, Baron went down to his supply clerk and asked for a bed tag. He filled it out with a fake name:

PFC Dave Williams. He made up the second bed, put a lock on the second wall locker, and when the platoon sergeant came around with a new roomie… Baron innocently asked if they were moving PFC Williams out. Confused, the platoon sergeant found somewhere else to house the new person, and Baron ended up with a private room.

Baron enjoyed his new living arrangement, but eventually the platoon sergeant grew concerned that he hadn't actually met PFC Williams. Every time anyone asked Baron about him, he had just headed to the latrine, or to a study group. Eventually, the company commander got involved in tracking this mysterious PFC down. They posted an order for PFC Williams to report to the commander on the daily Action Notice (a fancy Army term for a simple bulletin board). Everyone in the company had to read the Action Notice every day, and that included both SPC and PVT Dave Williams.

The two men showed up, and were called into the commander's office.

"Who are you?"

"Specialist Williams, sir."

"I asked for Private First Class Williams. Go to class, Specialist!"

"Yes, sir!"

"Who are you?"

"Private Williams, sir."

"You're not Private First Class?"

"No, sir, but I'd be happy to accept an early promotion!"

"Get the hell out of here! And if you see PFC Williams, tell him his ass is mine!"

This went on for several weeks.

Of course, the Korean language is very challenging—obviously, we all struggled with English, as well—and not everyone makes it through the course. SPC Baron failed three tests in a row and was reclassified into another job field. When he shipped out, he left an empty room, a perplexed commander, and a bed tag for PVT Dave Williams to use upon his eventual promotion.

Our little section was growing more friendly, but I still couldn't get a reaction out of that damned jarhead! I simply *had* to get him to let his guard down. His impervious demeanor felt like the one obstacle to my total sense of belonging there. My usual smart-aleck remarks and puns in class were no good. Steve ignored them, and the teachers didn't speak English well enough to get them. God forbid that they hear me and ask me to explain a joke.

Korean humor does not allow for the kinds of jokes I tell. Kenny Lee was the only member of the teaching team who could reliably recognize when I was joking, but he didn't often laugh. He was more likely to lecture us on the fact that you have to be a Level 2 linguist to understand humor, and since Level 2 was what we were expected to achieve at the end of the course, we were nowhere near earning the privilege. (This often led to him telling us about the sitcom pilot he was writing.)

But sometimes humor can't bridge the gulf between cultures, and even being Level 2 wouldn't change that. Take the assignment to translate a joke; should have been right up my alley, no? I tried one from my second grade joke books: Q: How do you catch a squirrel? A: Climb up a tree and act like a nut! (rimshot) It would help if Korean had a word for "nut" or "squirrel." My joke translated as, "How do you capture tree rats? Climb a tree and act like a crazy person." It was much funnier simply trying to get a Korean to say "squirrel."

Poor Mrs. Chong fell for that one. "Soo-kah-do-do. Ser-ko-laller. Sok-ho-lillah."

Never mind. Steve sat staring straight ahead even throughout that episode.

I tried all kinds of subtle tricks; I even tried stupid stunts. One day we were sitting in a line: me, Angie, Steve, and Dave. Angie blew a bubble with an illegal piece of gum while the teachers were in the hall between class periods, so I crowed, "Fire in the Hole!" and shot it with a rubber band. Gum shrapnel flew everywhere, and the rubber band landed on the desk in front of Dave. Dave shook his head in bewilderment and said, "I don't even want to know what you are thinking." Angie demanded a new piece of gum. It was, in a word hilarious, and the class lost it.

Steve had festive little pink balls strewn across his immaculate uniform, festooning his bristly crew cut, and littering his otherwise neat desktop. This *had* to be it! I expected something, even if it wasn't laughter; maybe rage, maybe ire. Anything to make him bend! His only reaction was to blandly brush his desk clear. I felt hopeless. I was ready to give up, and concede that I would never see into the soul of this fellow human being. It was, for me, a bitter kind of defeat.

But then my day arrived in the person of Mr. Minh.

Mr. Minh was a very special teacher. He was ancient in a way that only a Korean man can be ancient. He had a steel-wool mop of hair and a tweed jacket with leather patches at the elbows. He stood a stooped 4' 11" at most, and he was the only teacher to level with us when we asked insensitive, "ugly American" sorts of questions. Like the day he was asked if Korean people really eat dogs; while the other teachers blustered and denied it as slander, Mr. Minh simply shut the door (after checking to make sure the hallway was free of eavesdroppers) and said to us, "Listen. Yellow dog, most tender..." We had no idea whether he was kidding or not, but no one raised that question again for the rest of the year.

Mr. Minh was a new arrival on our teaching team. He had belonged to another class on the first floor that had graduated, and he was reassigned to us. He poked his head into the room during Mr. Park's class one day, and announced that he was going to need help moving his things up one flight of stairs. His "things" included a 1950's era, powder-blue metal desk. It must have weighed as much as a city bus. But what is the point of having stupid, young men around if you can't get them to volunteer to move a two-ton desk up a flight of stairs?

So, in order to get out of Mr. Park's class, a bunch of us went downstairs to help Mr. Minh: me, Steve, the two Dave Williams (SPC and PVT), and PVT Harris (a female soldier wanting to put us to shame).

Together we hefted the behemoth and trundled it to the stairwell. We somehow managed to work it through the door, and up to the first landing, but we had to lift it four feet up to work around the turn. The Daves were on the bottom, Steve and Harris were above, and I was guiding the side. It went well, until somehow the thing began to tilt; in slow motion, I watched as the desktop loomed, pressing me closer to the concrete block wall of the stairwell. When I realized that it was about to press my head into the wall... no, through the wall... I said something. Unfortunately, they didn't hear me, so I made more noise.

I do not recall what noise I made, but I imagine that it was the sound of an animal that the Korean people would have no problem eating. Steve looked around the corner of the desk to see what was the matter, and saw me being ground into USAF grade A dork flour. "Stop!" he bellowed, and the others stopped moving.

And then the corners of his mouth quirked up, and he uttered two sharp *heh*s.

Everyone else heard it, too. They all knew about my quest, of course. It's not like it was a secret. I think there was even a pool going on when/whether it would ever happen. Steve's double "heh" surely cost someone a six-pack of crappy beer. But at the time, no one said anything about it. They shifted the desk, removed the danger to my cranium, and finished the task at hand.

Once we were back in the room, there was no time to comment. Mr. Park was in full lecture mode, acting as though five sweaty young students had not just barged into the room. We tucked right into the lesson. The incident was not mentioned until break time, when Steve turned to Dave.

"Sir," he said, "I apologize for my loss of bearing."

Dave looked over at me and asked, "Are you alright?"

I was a little dazed, still, but I nodded.

"And have you learned anything," he asked me, pointedly.

"Yes," I said. "Marines like slapstick."

7

The Bachelor Party

(All names have been changed to protect the guilty. Except my own.)

The smoke deck was the focal point of social life for everyone in the squadron. Even people who didn't smoke would go there as soon as their duties were done for the day, just to put in an appearance. Some were fresh out of Basic Training and glad to spend their 20 minutes of freedom outside; some were "sharking," which involved circling amongst the newbies, looking for one that would be easily wowed by the seniority of someone who had been there for as long as three weeks already.

I know several young men who got their first dates this way.

I was one of those who went to smoke. I had never been more than a pack-a-week kind of guy, but just being able to go out and have a cigarette after eight weeks of stress and mind games was a temptation that I couldn't even think of resisting. Now it was October, a month after I had arrived at DLI, and I had acquired a couple of stogies to celebrate being allowed to wear civilian clothes again. I relished my flannel shirt and Detroit Tigers baseball cap (I've always been a big Magnum PI fan), and I had on a pair of jeans that seemed much looser than they had last time they were worn, four months before. Bert came up to me, took the cigar I offered, and said, "I got someone who wants to meet you."

Then she stepped out from behind him. "Hey, aren't you the guy that can put a quarter up his nose?" she said. She was the adorable girl I had been admiring while standing in formation for the last four weeks. And clearly Bert had been telling her about my favorite party trick.

"Got a quarter?" I replied dashingly. She laughed, and to make a long story short, by February we had decided to get married.

Of course, most of our friends were scandalized. After all, it was drilled into us by now that DLI marriages usually don't last more than six months beyond the end of the couple's stay in Monterey. The odds for a marriage like ours were not good. Maybe that explains why I was more nervous about telling people about the wedding than I had been proposing.

Most people who heard our happy news offered flaccid congratulations before moving on to more interesting subjects, and most of my close friends seemed worried when I told them. But not Glenn. He became visibly excited at the prospect, and his first words were, "Can I throw the bachelor party?" So I said sure.

When the big night arrived, we borrowed my fiancée's Saturn and swung by the liquor store on our way to the motel where the festivities would be held. Glenn had outdone himself. He'd secured a suite under the name "Nick Nefsik" (Arabic for "fuck yourself") which had a kitchenette, and a balcony overlooking the Chinese restaurant behind the motel.

People started to show up, and we all started to get blasted and watch porn. A typical night, for most of the guys, and a bit boring. Then someone suggested getting a stripper. Everyone ponied up a few bucks, and Don Law, whom everyone called "Dong," went to work with the phone book. She showed up about half an hour later with her bouncer; a beefy, sullen woman that stood in the corner of the room watching us watch her friend.

Thus the fun began...

And then there was a knock on the door. Apparently, there was an Air Force girl in the room next door with her boyfriend, an Army sergeant. I probably don't need to point out that their relationship was not legal, but I will; even if it was not adultery, he was considered "permanent party" assigned to the base, and she was a student—a student leader, in fact. They didn't see eye to eye on much, but the service commanders all agreed that this met the definition of fraternization under the United Code of Military Justice. This should have made the couple more discrete, but they were more upset about all the noise coming from our room.

The guy came to the door and demanded to know who the ranking NCO was at the party. Dong explained that there wasn't an NCO in charge of bachelor parties, but that the stripper would be leaving before 10:30 p.m. All we asked was a little patience. The guy seemed to agree, and left. Then he came back. His girlfriend wanted us quiet immediately, and sent him back to threaten to call the authorities... but no one bothered to hear him out this time, because the dancing was beginning, and the door was politely slammed in his face.

The stripper was quite good. She zeroed in on the bachelor (me, of course) and did a very naughty dance, which I wasn't able to fully appreciate because I had misplaced my glasses, and was totally obliterated. When she was done with that, she made a little pitch about needing extra money to play a game called "Feed the Kitty," after which everyone bolted from the hotel to find the nearest cash machine. This was fortunate for most of them. While we waited for the bank roll patrol to return, the stripper disappeared into the bathroom (where my roommate turned out to be hiding in the tub), and a few of the guys went out on the balcony for a smoke.

Fred Kreigler sat by the window staring myopically at the porno on the TV when he heard a knock on the window behind him. There were about a dozen guys still inside the room, and I was by the wall dividing the bedroom area from the kitchenette, when Fred pulled back the curtain to see a grinning Death's head with a chin divot and a hairline that was retreating like a Redskin's defensive line.

"It's Sergeant Knight!" he shouted... and mayhem ensued.

Technical Sergeant Everett Knight was in charge of the student leader program, and some of us considered him to be the person who was truly in charge of the squadron. He controlled a vast spy network with the green, yellow, and red ropes at his disposal, and there were rumors that his current wife was a former student—a severely improper relationship, if true. (Not that improper relationships weren't happening in the next room, of course.)

Stories of his cruelty and his retribution were whispered throughout the ranks. Some said he ate raw meat for breakfast; still others said he wore a mask made of the skin of students who washed out. With his pointed teeth—all of them, not just the bicuspids—and abyss of a chin-divot, his face was enough to inspire terror without any gory accoutrements, and whatever else may have been said about him, his appearance at my bachelor party meant that heads were about to roll.

I don't know who opened the door of the hotel room, because Kreigler swore later that it wasn't him. Maybe TSgt Knight really was the supernatural being we all thought he was and teleported through the wall. It's more likely that Kreigler had left the window open, and since it was right by the door, TSgt Knight simply reached in through the window and unlocked the door.

He burst through the door and grabbed as many people by the back of the shirt as he could reach. The stampede of retreating victims flowed by me in my place against the wall, and I stared stupidly into the panicked faces of my companions as they were chased down by the leering, gleeful avatar of retribution.

When the dust settled, there were about six of us left in the room with TSgt Knight, who looked around the room, smirking and braying threats into our faces. The Incarnation of Death was turning to each of us and trying to find out who had escaped his clutches by diving off the balcony.

"Who booked the room?" he shouted. "I want to know who Nick Nefsik is." We were trying to make it look like we couldn't remember, but we were really just trying to figure out who we would have to turn in. I remember reluctantly giving Glenn's name, but tried to make it sound better by pointing out that he hadn't bought alcohol for anyone but me.

After much soul-thrashing, we managed to come out with only five names of people we were pretty sure he'd already seen. He had to be satisfied with that. Then it occurred to our ranking NCO that one of our drunken runners might have been injured diving off that balcony, so he sent someone around to see.

Sure enough, the guy returned with Dong draped across his back. Dong looked around the room blearily, whether through pain, inebriation, or both. He looked hard at TSgt Knight for a few seconds, then burst out, "Who invited *this* asshole?"

We all froze, and our blood ran cold at the smile that crept across his malignant mug. TSgt Knight leaned back, took a deep breath (as we held ours)... and laughed! "You're alright, then, Airman Law?"

In the end, the party turned out pretty well. Nobody got into too much hot water, though a few of the people there had been student leaders and had their positions of responsibility taken away. Two under-age guys were put back "on phase," which meant they had to keep a curfew and stay in uniform all the time. But since TSgt Knight had ordered them to ride their motorcycles back from the hotel, he couldn't very well charge them with any legal action.

Most importantly, my wedding went on as planned. My lovely new bride was mad that I had worried her, but I was forgiven for not actually causing any damage to either our plans or her car. Fortunately, I had been able to convince our apprehender that I should stay at the motel that night, since I was unable to drive.

Glenn showed up after everyone had been dragged off, and he helped me clean up the room.

"I'm sorry your bachelor party got busted," he said.

"I'm sorry I ratted you out," I said.

"That's alright. Everyone knew I'd set it up; someone would have told on me," he forgave me.

"Where were you, anyway?" I asked. "How did you get away?"

"Well, when everyone else was going off the balcony, me and Duke hopped over the dividing wall to the balcony of the room next door. We lit up a couple of smokes, and just watched. TSgt Knight didn't notice us, so we slid down the drain pipe. I've been at another party down at the other end of the motel." Typical Glenn!

And the chick that turned us in? The one with the Army sergeant boyfriend? We made sure everyone knew she and her boyfriend had made the call to TSgt Knight... including her husband.

8
Politically Incorrect (Doesn't Cover It)

I think the statute of limitations for having a bad attitude has run out by now. I hope so, because I have found physical evidence of my bad attitude. If I recall correctly, it was our teacher, Kenny Lee, who showed us a video on Korean culture one day (in Korean, of course, so I understood none of it) and asked us to take notes as we watched it.

Here are my some of my notes:

"While it may seem that Koreans borrowed art and customs from China and Japan, and borrowed their music from an African tribe which communicates solely through farts and tap dancing, Koreans do have some practices which are solely their own. For example, on some holidays they try to coax dead relatives out of their burial mounds with plates of rotten cabbage."

"When they want to celebrate, they get drunk and tie streamers to their heads and dash about the town beating pots and pans. Sometimes people are accidentally killed by the streamers, which gives those who were annoyed by the celebration cause to celebrate in a like manner, which sometimes leads to a month-long stretch of perpetual noise and accidental streamer-decapitation."

"Koreans have a worldwide reputation for their dog-training technique; if only those damned dogs would learn!"

I tried to keep my opinions mostly to myself, though I probably made my friend Angie read this particular screed. Even I recognized that this baldly racist treatment of a whole people was wholly inappropriate, but I was also very angry that I had been stuck in Korean class at all, and that I was doing so badly in the class.

I was something of an aberration, as most of my classmates were excited about being there. The only officer in our class was an Army captain who had married a Korean woman and wanted to be able to relate to his in-laws. A few of the Army privates had relatives who had served in the Korean War, or some other long-held desire to learn the language. Their eagerness sometimes led to unintentional offensiveness, as when they learned that the Arabic students had all been assigned "Arab names" to use in class. They badgered the Korean teachers to assign us Korean names, but names are apparently more personal in Korean culture, and the teaching team told us they had to get to know us so they could give us appropriate names.

They did give the captain a name: "Bong-nam Dei-wi," which they translated as "Captain Happy Man." Feeling left out, a couple of the guys took matters into their own hands and wrote up their own name tags. "Wun Hung Lo" and "Way Big Sack" thought they were very clever until Mr. Lee walked in and commented, "Those sound like Chinese names. That's not very authentic."

Our teachers were an interesting bunch. Mr. Nam was introduced to us as the head of the teaching team on the first day by the Chief Military Language Instructor, or MLI. Mr. Minh was the eldest of the teachers, and his English was stilted and formal. Even though everyone kept up the pretense that he was in charge, it was Kenny Lee who seemed to run things. Mr. Park was not the most fluent English speaker of the bunch, but he had a sense of humor closer to our own which made it easier to relate to him. At least, we assumed he was joking when he insisted that we call him "Pharoah" and threatened to slit our throats for turning in late assignments, or for making him homesick by using the word for a coffee house: "da-bang."

Mrs. Song and Mrs. Chung were very sweet, but their English was abysmal. Mrs. Song had a flair for presentation, and at least tried to sound like she understood us. Her classes often felt like a stage production, but it quickly became apparent that she neither understood us when we spoke to her nor knew whether we understood her. Mrs. Chung only ever seemed to say, "Risten to ta-puh, and-uh repeat-uh," before pressing play on our language exercise tapes. I know that rendering her speech that way is rude, but I learned from trying to talk to her that imitating the way someone sounds in English can actually help you perfect the way to pronounce that person's language. That one little trick probably did as much to keep my grades afloat as anything else.

Kenny Lee definitely had the advantage of the other teachers when it came to speaking English. He told us he had been in America for 18 years, and he did pick up on more of our in-jokes and references than the others. He was proud of his skills and told anyone who would listen about his ambition to sell his sitcom pilot to some studio in Los Angeles.

Yet, despite his advanced ability, he still couldn't pronounce English letters like "V" or "F" very well. This combined with the very Korean culture of our teaching team created some deep, insurmountable problems for me. Specifically, the Korean notion that a teacher is the fountain of wisdom, and the student's job is to quietly sip that wisdom from delicate cups without making a fuss.

Every class at DLI has an MLI: a military language instructor with some experience actually doing the linguist mission. The MLIs do teach class, but their main function is to act as a bridge between the native speakers and the boisterous, sometimes intolerant young students. Our MLI was an army sergeant first class by the name of Travis Lowell. SFC Lowell was a tall, occasionally friendly African-American man who had taught himself Korean while stationed in Osan as a mechanic.

SFC Lowell labored to explain the Korean concepts of status and respect to us, often in vain. It sounds simple enough to say that one should always respect one's elders, but knowing what would be considered "disrespectful" proved to be much more elusive, especially for a sarcastic person like me. As I tried to weather the turbulent water between the waves of badly communicated instruction and the rocky shores of Korean propriety, I learned to my disgust that there was no occasion in which I would ever be in the right.

Example: Kenny Lee presented one lesson to us in which he wrote a number of examples on the chalkboard, and underlined pieces of the words explaining that we needed to be able to pick out the "bobostem" in each word. He kept saying that, over and over, and I looked at the others to see if they were as lost as I was. Some seemed to be confused, others simply nodded and kept their faces placid.

I tried asking what he meant, but Mr. Lee didn't like the way I phrased my questions and shouted, "You don't question me! I am teacher, and you are student! You sit and be quiet or you won't learn!"

Chastened, I stopped asking questions. For weeks, he would mention "bobostem" and I was just as confused as on that first day; but I didn't ask any questions. Finally, someone in the class got it. "He can't say his v's," they whispered to the rest of the class. "He's saying 'verb stem'!"

That realization helped, but my grades for that unit were shot by that point. When I got my grade report, Mr. Lee had written in the comment section that went to my flight leader, "A1C Callin needs to participate more in class, and ask more question."

This was the life I lead in Korean class. My squadron was not happy to see that comment, either, and made sure I understood that failing out of the class due to a Lack of Effort was prosecutable under the Unified Code of Military Justice. The UCMJ was the Bible as far as military discipline was concerned, and if they threatened to apply it to you, you knew you were in for it.

The class was 14 modules of instruction, scheduled for 63 weeks, and we were barely a third of the way in. I didn't want to be there, I didn't understand the teachers, I didn't appreciate the culture or the language—and the only other option was prison. So when Kenny Lee gave us our next assignment for that weekend, that's where my head was.

The assignment was to write three sentences in Korean about our hometown. My hometown is Phoenix, so I tried to come up with three quick sentences made up of words that I knew. There weren't a lot. "Phoenix is big." One down. "Phoenix is hot." On a roll! Now what? I thought for a long time, but nothing really came to mind. Then, a flash of genius: "I love Phoenix because there are no Koreans there. Just kidding."

Yes, I looked up "just kidding," and put that in there, too.

In retrospect, it wasn't a really good move.

Mr. Lee collected our assignments and stood skimming through them before starting class, and I knew right away when he saw mine. His face reddened, and he dragged me out the door and into his office, which was really just a cubby separated from the classroom by a thin, fabric wall, and proceeded to rip me a new one. "This is racist stuff, you know? You could be prosecuted for this! I don't know if you're trying to be funny, but you gotta be a Level 2 at least before you try humor! Like me, I gotta Level 2 in English, and that's why I write a pilot for a sitcom. Have I let you read it?"

I struggled mightily not to let my eyes roll. Level 2 was the minimum we needed to achieve on the Defense Language Proficiency Test in order to graduate. It was a scale of one to five, with Level 5 being a Ph.D.-educated native speaker and Level 0 being someone with no knowledge of the language whatsoever. Most high school kids who slouch their way through a two-year Spanish class probably rate about Level 0+ at best. It was my judgment that Mr. Lee was a little too proud of his Level 2 in English, but I knew now would not be a good time to bring that up.

"It's funny... about a used car lot, because, you know, they get different people in every day, and some of them are probably crazy." He was still talking about his script. "But if I see this kind of racist stuff go on, you will get in big trouble. Now go back to class!"

Chastised and chagrined, I crept meekly back to my seat. I knew the rest of the class had heard every word, and I felt two inches tall.

Humiliated and wronged, I sat staring intently at the tip of my pencil until Mr. Lee came back into the room to continue our lesson.

"Today, I write a Korean sentence on the board, and you try to figure it out from context." He scribbled something up there, and we puzzled over it, feverishly flipping through our dictionaries. The only word I could make out looked like "hug-in," which the dictionary defined as, "a Negro; a darkie; a coon..." I sat back, put down my pencil, and waited silently for one of our three "hug-in" students to notice.

When they did, the class had a very calm, rational discussion about how the word was really a technical term, on a par with "African-American" or "person of color." Once the tensions were allayed, someone thought to ask what the rest of the sentence meant.

"Oh, it say, 'Black people are lousy tippers.'" The temperature dropped 10 degrees. "What, that not racist! That true! You go into restaurant, they eat and eat, but don't leave anything on table. It just observation!"

Captain Happy Man got everyone to calm down, and we tried to appeal to SFC Lowell to explain to Mr. Lee that his remarks were out of line, but instead SFC Lowell tried to explain to us that this was "just how Koreans were."

"The right way to deal with them is to be overly polite," he suggested. "When I was stationed in Osan, I'd been speaking the language for a while, and I got on a bus. I sat next to an old lady who started making comments to her friends about how badly the 'big American hug-in' stank and suggesting that maybe I planned to ride to Africa. But rather than get mad, I stood up, and bowed, and said in Korean, 'Honored grandmother, I will be happy to give up my seat if I offend you.'

"She lost a lot of face because she and her friends realized I could understand them, and she immediately got off the bus. I ended up with that whole seat to myself!"

In light of the complicated attitude toward racism, I did my best to dial back any attempts at humor. I started focusing on what proved to be an impossible task: making sure I was clearly understood.

SFC Lowell's deference to the teaching team went beyond tolerating their baser cultural impulses. Several of the teachers had trouble making themselves understood when it came to assigning homework. There were multiple occasions when a whole section of the class would fail to turn in an assignment because the teacher either forget to assign it, or did so in Korean, and no one understood their instructions.

The third time this happened with our section in a two week period, SFC Lowell burst into the room and threatened everyone with an Article 15. Article 15 of the UCMJ was a way for a commander to punish troops for minor infractions. The Army students in the class received them all the time for things like failing room inspections, but the Air Force reserved them for actual crimes, like a DUI or being charged with assault in a bar fight.

When we figured out what he was angry about, we tried to explain to him that no one had assigned the lesson he was angry about, and that an Article 15 was more severe than he probably intended it to be for the Air Force people. He scowled at us, focusing particularly on the airmen in the classroom, and growled, "I don't know what you're up to, but I've got a real case of the ass with this class!"

That comment sent us into hysterics—once he left the room, of course—and a mysterious hand-drawn flier advertising an effective ass salve appeared on SFC Lowell's desk that afternoon.

I wish I'd managed to save a copy of that instead of my anti-Korean class notes. It was definitely Level 2 humor, at very least.

9
The Drunk

Anyone who spent any time at DLI in the mid-90s may have heard the stories of A1C Bruce Archer. He was well-regarded by everyone who knew him, but he did have one little personality quirk: in a squadron of 700+ college-age military trainees, he was a notorious drinker.

The vast majority of our student body liked to party, but he stood out. When other people would go to the bars in town, they would typically order a beer or cider to start off. Some of the heavy hitters might go straight to shots. But Archer would order two pitchers, then turn to whomever he was with and ask, "Are you having anything to drink tonight?"

Generally speaking, he didn't let this habit affect his Air Force career. Maybe I would be more accurate to say he didn't let the Air Force interfere with his drinking career. You could guarantee that every night, from Friday to Sunday, he was going to be publicly intoxicated. Holidays and "Blood Days"—we were given a day off from class if we donated to the periodic blood drives—would allow him to extend his drinking time further into the week. And while the rest of us had to keep a watchful eye out to make sure we weren't caught by student leaders, who were charged with the unofficial task of writing us up for drinking too much or inadvertently buying drinks for under-aged friends, Archer seemed immune to them.

The collection of Drunken Archer stories grew over his vast tenure at DLI, especially as he was repeatedly rolled back in his class.

Usually people were only rolled back once, either for academic reasons or in rare cases, for medical reasons. "Rolling back" meant that if they couldn't keep up, they would get transferred into a class that was two months or more behind theirs in the same language program. Archer was rolled back the first time because he had an undescended testicle that the USAF had decided must be removed. This extended his stay at DLI by several months, and then he ran into academic trouble as he struggled with the material. They decided that the Air Force had invested enough resources in him by this point, they would go ahead and roll him back a second time to let him catch up. By the end of his time at DLI, he had been there for more than two years, and attended an unprecedented three Chinese courses.

Meanwhile, his adventures with alcohol continued. His favorite trick was to get himself obliterated and then evacuate himself in some inappropriate place. When Archer was drunk, he would piss and crap anywhere, as the spirit moved him. Pun intended. His squad-mates complained to him frequently about not urinating in the flight laundry room. One exasperated bay chief went so far as to ask him to use the washing machine, as it was easier to clean than the dryer. This led to a knock on that bay chief's door in the middle of the night: it was Archer, asking for some laundry soap so he could "flush."

Perhaps his greatest moment came when he was staggering up the hill from the Enlisted Club one Saturday night and felt his bowels beginning to move. He was on the tennis courts, halfway up to the squadron from the E-Club; he couldn't go back there, since they had just closed. He didn't think he'd make it up the hill, and he didn't fancy squatting there in the open on a moonlit night. So he did what anyone in his position would have done: he snuck into one of the front yards of the officers' quarters that bordered the tennis courts.

As he did his business behind a bush under the picture window, he noticed that the car parked out front looked familiar, and he squinted at the name on the mailbox: J. Gallegos. He was shitting in the Air Force commander's yard. He proudly told a captivated audience this tale while sitting on my couch at a party sometime later, and then promptly fell into a deep sleep. We, of course, rolled him outside to keep him from taking a dump in our oven, or someplace even worse.

One weekend, just before the monthly Monday morning inspection, his roommate, A1C Waldo, was livid. It was Sunday night, and Archer was still, typically, MIA, presumably at the Mucky Duck or Characters. Waldo had to clean the whole room by himself. Okay, he didn't *have* to, but he thought he'd fail the inspection if Archer's junk was scattered all over the place. He piled Archer's things in his own locker, swept, mopped and waxed the floor, and collapsed, exhausted, sometime after midnight.

At 0300, Archer was poured out of a cab, and the dorm guard on duty rousted Jones, the flight commander, and another poor sap—both were student leaders, I must point out—to drag Archer down the hall to his room. As they did so, he woke up and began flailing about. He only settled down after bouncing his head off the laundry room door knob.

They pounded on his door, waking a disoriented Waldo. They all dumped Archer on his bed (the bottom bunk, fortunately) and Waldo attempted to get back to sleep. Just as he drifted off, he heard something and turned on the light.

He saw Archer standing in the middle of the room, spraying copious amounts of urine over all of their shoes, which Waldo had lined up neatly along the wall under the window. Waldo launched out of the top bunk, pummeled Archer on the back, and shoved him toward the door, shrieking, "No, you stupid bastard! Get out of here to do that!"

So, Archer opened the door to the room and gamely obliged by whizzing out into the hallway. He finished as Waldo danced a jig of rage behind him, and then lay back down to sleep—on his desk.

The desks were side by side against the wall, so while Archer was trying to rest his banged-up head on his desk, his feet were on Waldo's. The problem here was that Waldo had a shelf unit on his desk, which was loaded with books and language tapes, knick-knacks and CDs, and other neatly tidied junk that tended to accumulate on such shelves. In his thrashing to get comfortable, Archer kicked the whole mess onto the floor.

Hearing the crash, Waldo rushed back into the room from the hallway, where he had been frantically mopping up piss with a pair of socks. He screamed again, heaved Archer from the desktop, and threw him onto his bed, from which he did not budge for three and one half hours.

Those hours saw Waldo reassembling his desk shelf and re-shelving all of his stuff; cleaning urine out of his shoes; re-mopping, re-waxing, and re-buffing the floor of his room and the entire length of the hallway. (He would have only done the pissy places, but his screaming had awakened his squad leader, who assigned him the whole hallway as "punishment for causing a disturbance.")

At 0549, Waldo finally finished cleaning and went to try to shower and get ready in time for the 0600 inspection. Alas, the cleaning detail had already finished cleaning the showers, and he was kept out. Thus, he stood inspection in an unkempt, unshaven, and smelly state, having been spattered with urine, sweat, and floor wax during the night.

As TSgt Beale was writing up Waldo's inspection paperwork, Archer came staggering out of the room, clutching his head. The side of his head behind his ear had swollen so badly that you could see straight into his ear while looking him in the eye.

"Airman Archer," said TSgt Beale, "are you alright?"

"No, sir," replied Archer. "I think I hit my head last night." He looked every inch the victim of some horrible assault.

"You'd better get to sick call, right away!"

Waldo watched him leave through a gauntlet of sympathy for his wounds, and slowly ground his teeth at the injustice—sick call exempted Archer from inspection.

Two days later, Waldo volunteered to become a student leader. Those of us closest to him were shocked; he had always complained loudest about the student leaders and the way the staff used them to spy on off-duty airmen. He made the most fun of his friends when they got their ropes, goose-stepping around them and shouting orders in an offensive parody of a Prussian officer.

Asked why he suddenly wanted to be a student leader—people whom he had taken to calling "student Nazis"—he said simply, "Revenge."

10
Piggies

Upon her arrival in California, Lieutenant Colonel Harriet J. Gallegos set out to make things better in her new command. She met with her staff, and received orders from the wing commander, and contemplated all of the things that needed to change. Her predecessor had been a friend to the airmen in his squadron, but that clearly was not a good approach, as discipline and good order were needed to stamp out the rampant smoking, drinking, and sexual escapades of her student body. Everywhere she looked there examples of lax standards, loose morals, and evidence that these Generation X slackers needed her guiding hand in their lives.

But before getting down to the business of implementing her program, she took a trip with her family to Santa Cruz and spent the day on their famous boardwalk. They rode rides and played carnival games, and she won a great, spherical, pink plush pig—which gave her a wonderful, horrible, awful idea.

My lovely bride, Kate, and I had already come to the attention of "Aunt Harry," and not in the best way. There had been a number of people lined up outside the commander's door for punishment after my infamous bachelor party, for one. And then, on the very day of our wedding, a Friday afternoon normally reserved for a 30-minute commander's call between the wings, our 700-member squadron was split into male and female groups and led to separate showings of a 20-minute abstinence training video. We sat quietly through the program, and when it was over, TSgt Knight asked if we had any questions.

"Yeah, sir," I said, "will you be sending a student leader to enforce this while I'm on my honeymoon?"

No. The answer was no.

The commander had a number of bad ideas. One of my favorites lasted fewer than three weeks: the Student Chaplain program. There are a lot of things about an airman's daily life that are up to commander's discretion in the rule book. Lt Col Gallegos used her discretion to ban smoking on the Presidio, but quickly learned that the post commandant, a grouchy Army colonel, happened to be a prolific smoker, and she was reminded (with several full-throated vodka- and Marlboro-scented obscenities) that it was not within her power to ban smoking on his post. So it became part of the student leaders' duties to enforce a no-smoking rule among the airmen. They were also the enforcers of tighter rules about drinking (no alcohol from Sunday night through Friday afternoons), monitors of travel (no leaving a 50-mile radius of DLI without approved leave forms), and local area activities (no one was allowed to rent a hotel room within 50 miles of DLI).

After a very brief time under this new regime, tempers became frayed and incidents of bad behavior began popping up with alarming frequency. The Student Chaplain program was something the commander thought of while reading (what else) *Chicken Soup for the Soul*. She laid out her vision of "students helping each other with their spiritual needs," and asked for volunteers at one of her Friday commander's calls. These spiritual leaders would wear a white rope and be considered student leaders.

By the next Friday, she had five volunteers: a Muslim Arabic student, two Mormons, a Wiccan, and a Buddhist. She reminded everyone that morale was low and improving each other's spiritual fitness was a good way to help raise it. By the Friday after that, the commander, who was a Roman Catholic, canceled the program, saying tersely that no one had taken her idea seriously.

Kate was horribly allergic to cigarette smoke, and was under 21, so my drinking and smoking were naturally being curbed anyway; and as a married couple, we applied to be moved onto F Flight. We received a modest three-bedroom house on Fort Ord. This eliminated our need to find accommodations that subverted the commander's de facto abstinence encouragement plan. Besides, setting up house together was such a blast, we didn't have much time for partying.

One thing we had done for a while was volunteer as PT monitors. Every day after school, we would change into running gear and meet up with A Flight—remember, they were the Phase One airmen, and they were required to run for their mandatory PT. We were on Phase Four, which meant we could manage our own exercise program, but we decided that it would be easier to maintain our practice if we ran on the same schedule as the newer folks.

The downside of being a PT monitor was that when we had new people fresh from Basic Training in the formation, they weren't used to running on Monterey's steep hills, and whenever those people fell out of formation with cramps or other issues, it was the job of a PT monitor to stay with them and make sure they made it back to the squadron safely. Unfortunately for me, this usually meant that instead of running the two miles, I was walking next to someone who didn't know what shin splints felt like, telling them to keep breathing and stop crying.

This, combined with my sedentary days in the classroom, meant that I was putting on a little weight. Strangely, Kate was too, even though she had an incredibly high metabolism and had been eating less since moving out to Fort Ord, probably due to the stress of getting to school on time upsetting her stomach in the morning.

"I don't like this," she would say, dressing in the morning. "My boobs are getting squashy." I never complained about that.

But, as I was contemplating other PT options I realized that Fort Ord was an easy bike ride from the Presidio, and with a convenient bike path leading from the bottom of Private Bolio Road where it intersected with Lighthouse Avenue all the way through Seaside, I decided to resign as a PT monitor, buy a bicycle, and make that 40-minute journey twice a day.

That's when the commander announced her pig idea.

"Good morning, squadron!" she crowed at us, holding the ridiculous pink toy under her arm. It clashed horribly with the Air Force blue of her uniform. "I've been noticing that morale is low, and some of you airmen are starting to look like little piggies!"

We braced ourselves for the worst. Last time she had mentioned low morale, one of our less popular airmen had pointed out that there were plaques in Commander's Hallway celebrating past Drill Competitions, and we had subsequently been required to show up for marching practice at 0700 on Saturday mornings. The airman in question had, naturally, washed out of her Vietnamese course and departed for another training school, so I'm sure the early drill practice improved her morale immensely.

"Since not enough of you are doing your own PT, I'm going to institute a weekly squadron run," the commander continued, as our peers from the other branches of service casually slowed their pace to hear every word. "Each Monday, you will all gather by flights, and we'll run the circuit around the whole post. That's just under two miles, all the way down the hill and all the way back up! As you run, we'll sing cadence, and throw this pig!" She brandished the pig over her head triumphantly as the horde of giggling Navy, Army, and Marine eavesdroppers scattered to tell their comrades what the Air Force was up to this week.

"If anyone drops the pig, we'll have to go around again, so look sharp, everyone!"

Kate and I went that weekend and bought bikes. On Monday, I let the flight commander running the PT monitor program know that I wouldn't be joining them the rest of the week. I had to assure her that I wasn't quitting because of the pig, and since we were all required to be there that afternoon, I would help out with my normal duties on these Monday runs.

It was a brilliant, rare sunny day, but the 700 faces assembled in their drab running gear looked miserable. We were spread out, doing stretches and some calisthenics while watching the double doors leading from Commander's Hallway. And then she appeared, the pig tucked under her arm, striding with her odd smile to the front of the formation.

We formed up. We snapped to when called to attention. We marked time, then began double time. The enormous, shuffling mass lurched around the corner and onto the road.

And the pig soared high into the air.

The first few people held onto the pig before launching it into the sky again, but then others began flinging it straight back, and it practically rolled across several hundred hands to the end of the line, like Eddie Vedder crowd-surfing at a Pearl Jam concert. Once at the back, someone was tapped to sprint to the front again with the pink monstrosity and begin the process anew.

As we ran, all of the other services turned out along the road to watch us go by. The commander acted as though they were cheering us, as if our squadron had returned from the front after licking Hitler, instead of jeering at a bunch of losers whose commander thought they were too fat to deserve dignity.

There was one close moment when someone fumbled, and we thought the pig was going to touch the ground. It may have, actually, but everyone denied that the black foot-shaped smudge was the result of an angry stomp, and the commander didn't press the issue. So, humiliated and sweaty, we returned to our starting point, and dispersed to our quarters to wash, change, and prepare to face the rest of the U.S. military at dinner. Hopefully there wouldn't be pork on the menu.

That week, I began my regimen of biking to school. The ride was amazing. I had the perfect riding mix (Dave Matthews Band, Spin Doctors, and Blues Traveler) on the Walkman, and whether I was going to school or back home, the trip started with a thrilling downhill half mile, followed by a peaceful beach cruise, and a half mile uphill workout.

Poor Kate seemed to be having a harder time with her stomach, and it was difficult to say whether the stress of her Arabic class was affecting her, or whether the nausea and occasional dizziness was affecting her work. Either way, her grades were slipping, and she was not happy. When she hadn't improved over the weekend, she finally agreed to visit the clinic—conveniently for her on Monday afternoon.

The Squadron Run started out about the same as the first one had, except the overcast sky did a better job of reflecting the mood of the squadron. There seemed to be a lot more spectators lined up on the road this week, and the commander beamed proudly as she strutted to the head of the column.

But this time, just as we got to the road, a small squad of Marines, carrying their platoon's guidon (the pole that every military unit uses to display ribbons and honors), charged from between the Marine and Navy buildings and plunged into the middle of our formation. They speared the pig, which was in mid-fling, on the chrome spear-point of their guidon, grunted a bellowing shout of "HOO-AH!" and barreled out of sight down the hill before any of the airmen thought to stop running.

"Get them!" shrieked the commander. "Get that pig back, now!"

The crowd had shuffled to a halt and was milling about in a mix of mirth and befuddlement. A couple of people trotted off to follow the Marines half-heartedly, but by now it was apparent that no one was sad to see the pig go.

Well, one person was. Lt Col Gallegos stood weeping in the road and staring around at our blank, unhelpful faces, as it dawned on her that we would have been happy to let the Marines carry *her* off, speared on their guidon. She stalked back to her office without another word.

Kate met up with us as we returned, and in retrospect, I shouldn't have been surprised by what she had to say. It made me forget about pigs, unhappy commanders, and intrusive student leader programs. All of the symptoms were there, and the timing was right, but it took a trip to the clinic for the truth to occur to either of us.

"Tad," she said, "I'm gonna be a momma!"

11
Pregnancies

Over the next several weeks, there was a bizarre change in the atmosphere of the squadron. Kate and I were over the moon with our happy news, and we didn't pay much attention to what was going on with everyone else. We only told a few people, not wanting to make a big deal about it until we were further along, but those we told were thrilled for us.

Meanwhile, Lt Col Gallegos was going through some dark times. She had been obliviously happy about her job before the incident with the pig, while the student body quietly and angrily stewed about her treatment of them; now there was a spiteful spring in everyone's step while she withdrew and tried to figure out how things went so wrong. To add insult to injury, the Marines began sending pieces of the pig to her office along with ransom notes composed from letters cut out of newspaper and magazine headlines. They were clearly trying to strike up a morbidly friendly rivalry, like the running feud they had with their Navy colleagues.

The Navy and Marine building was next door to the Air Force building, and had the Navy in the wing on the far side, with the Marines on the near side. The Navy kept an enormous anchor from a World War II ship in a memorial garden in front of their wing, which the Marines would paint pink every year on the anniversary of the founding of the Marine Corps. The Navy tried various ways to get revenge, up to and including the time they defaced the Marine's chin-up bars, which were out in front of their wing. Their posts had the slogan, "Pain is

Temporary/Pride is Forever" burned into them, one phrase on each vertical post, and the Navy stole over in the night and painted the word "Anal" over the first phrase and "Gay" over the second.

This had not gone over well, as you can imagine. But the Navy and Marine commanders had eventually worked out a truce. Now the Air Force commander was upset over the torture and dismemberment of her stuffed pig, and the Marine commander was having trouble taking her seriously.

He was not the only one. Upon learning that she now had eight pregnant airmen in her squadron, Lt Col Gallegos had decided that she needed to Do Something. She summoned all eight to her conference room, and informed them that they would be attending regular meetings with her during the duration of their pregnancies, as they clearly needed counseling. She refused to say so outright, but it was clear that she considered all eight pregnant airmen to be completely irresponsible, and her "counseling" was intended to shame them and deter others from choosing to follow their path. Never mind the fact that seven of the eight were married, and all had intentionally chosen the unusually long training environment for their gestation. I was not privy to the actual words exchanged, but it was clear to me that there was no love lost between Aunt Harry and these eight airmen.

There were also no follow-up counseling sessions.

For my part, I kept muddling through my classes, trying to stay out of trouble. The rule was that if a student failed three modules in a row, they were out. I kept squeaking by, failing one or two, then passing one or two. At least my mood was improving, as my habit of biking had allowed me to drop 11 pounds in the first month, and I was feeling great. I loved my morning rides. Of course, there was a bit of drama with that, too.

I don't know that this was related to Kate's run-in with the commander at her Naughty Pregnant Girl meeting, but out of the blue, I was tapped for a random weigh-in. I had lost weight, but they still weren't happy that I was "at the top of the allowable zone," so they taped me to measure my Body Mass Index. I know now that the BMI is not a useful tool the way they were applying it, I did not know this at the time. They measured my neck (where I had lost some of my weight) and my thigh (which daily cycling had enlarged) and announced that my mass was 26 percent fat. That meant I was two percent over the maximum, and I was placed in the USAF Weight Management Program.

At DLI, the Weight Management Program was run by a senior airman known as "Senior Airman Butterball" by the student body. He had been a staff sergeant, but had lost a stripe under the WMP, and had been assigned to Monterey while the Air Force went through the process of kicking him out of the service on a medical discharge. I tried to explain to him that I had begun biking and lost a lot of weight, but he ignored me and ordered me to report to Phase One PT, effective immediately. And, by the way, since I was going to be there anyway, would I be interested in resuming my PT monitor duties?

The quarterly PT tests were coming up, which meant that everyone in the squadron had to run a two-mile course around Soldier Field. I knew I was being manipulated into helping get the newbies in the squadron ready for that run, but there wasn't much I could do about it. I decided to suck it up, do the extra walking session that was PT monitoring, and keep riding my bike.

And then we got the sad news at Kate's twelve-week checkup that the baby was not moving. They ran tests and confirmed that she was no longer going to be a momma. They also noticed some "unusual cells" during their exam, and suggested scheduling an appointment to run a biopsy. Kate asked a lot of good questions while I just sat there. I hadn't really expected her to get pregnant right away, and until she was, I hadn't really thought about how much I wanted to be a dad. Now we were not only losing the baby, but despite their calm and reassuring way of putting it, we were facing the prospect of those unusual cells turning out to be something that would take away Kate.

Needless to say, none of this helped our academic performance. Between the stress and the exhaustion from the extra physical activity, I wore myself out and caught one of my tremendous head colds. The clinic was notorious for treating every ailment with ibuprofen and bed rest, but in my case they decided to prescribe a cough suppressant... and sent me back to class. I complained that the bright orange label indicated I would be drowsy, and the nurse just sneered, in a thick German accent, "Ve do not prescribe medication which vill make you drowsy!"

I nearly fell out the second-story window of our classroom trying to stay awake, and got sent home to rest.

Fortunately, I was well in time for the big PT test. Kate showed up in civilian clothes, having established that her PT waiver from the pregnancy covered her for six weeks *after* the fetus had passed. She'd had a crash course in miscarriage lore and legal issues, and she was handling it all in a most businesslike and professional manner. The commander hadn't been very polite about the whole thing, but she had stopped short of actually saying, "I told you so," and had left for a Temporary Duty Assignment (or a TDY, if you prefer).

As I stretched my legs and prepared for the run, Kate waved me over with a look of concern. "That's Mary Cowell," she said. "She was one of the Naughty Eight. Why is she on the field?" Mary was one of the married students, but she had been an A Flight student leader, so she was under a different flight sergeant that we were. It turned out she had miscarried also, and been told that if she wasn't pregnant, she had to run the PT test.

"That's wrong!" Kate protested, but Mary didn't want to rock the boat. When the PT test began, she started running. I kept pace with Mary, watching her carefully, and she ran slower and slower as she completed the first lap. She started to stumble and I knew there was trouble. There were PT monitors stationed around the field, and I sent one to get help.

We found Mary's husband in the group, but his sergeant was threatening to put him on Weight Management if he fell out, so he had to keep running as the ambulance arrived and took Mary off. When we finished the run, he sprinted off the field without waiting to hear his time. I went to Kate, who was shaking with rage and cursing about authoritarian pricks under her breath.

She strode up to Mary's flight sergeant, and without raising her voice, she got in his face and said, "A pregnancy waiver covers a woman until six weeks after the fetus *leaves her body*. 'Miscarriage' occurs when the fetus dies, and describes her condition until she *passes* the fetus. When you don't know what the rules are about something, you had better fucking ask. You just made someone miscarry on Soldier Field because you were too ignorant and lazy to ask a question."

He did not contradict her.

Kate had two appointments, a few weeks apart; the first to remove the fetus, and the second for a cryosurgical biopsy. She had to heal from the first before they could perform the second. In between, both of us continued to worry and to struggle in class.

I was back to only one failure, having passed a test two weeks prior, and I was looking forward to a three-day weekend. My friend Angie, who had become close friends with Kate, too, was a frequent guest at our house, and we often let her stay in our unused third bedroom. The plan this weekend was to let Angie have the run of our house while we took a small trip down the Pacific Coast Highway together.

Angie and I had both failed that last test, which meant that after the rest of the class was dismissed for the day, we had to attend a "seventh hour" study hall. Mrs. Song was our teacher for this study hall that day, and she seemed eager to start the long weekend, too. She usually spoke in flowery, meandering sentences, and we did our best to make sense of them. On this day, it took her several tries to make us understand that she was letting us go early.

"Is there homework?" we asked.

"No homework!" she smiled.

And we took her at her word. Angie had to fetch her things and I went to find Kate and the car. I was chatting with some friends on the smoke deck when I saw SFC Lowell and Angie, still in her uniform, striding into the commander's front door. I ran over and followed them into the building in time to hear SFC Lowell telling our first sergeant that we had ditched seventh hour and failed to complete our homework. He was demanding that the Shirt track me down when I walked up and asked what was going on.

"You airmen think you're so clever, huh?" he snapped. "Well, I'm going to push for an Article 15 on this one, you can just bet!" This set the first sergeant's teeth on edge, having someone from another branch of service usurp her disciplinary authority in front of her, but she didn't say anything to contradict him. Instead, we were told to return to the classroom with SFC Lowell.

We walked out of the building with him, and I told him I needed to let my wife know that Angie and I were going to be late. He eyed us with some amusement, and said, "Yeah, I heard about you all. Got quite the hot three-way action going on at the Callin house, don't you?"

Angie stopped walking. She got quiet, and calm, and asked him what he meant. He told her. It was lewd. And there were witnesses, right there on the smoke deck. Angie smiled, and asked him to return to the first sergeant with her.

The first sergeant was not impressed with his behavior, or his remarks. Sexual harassment was a relatively new idea for him, but not for a female first sergeant. Seeing him treat her airmen that way gave her reason to doubt his other accusations; if he was prone to abusing his position, she wasn't going to entertain anything questionable from him. He was sent on his way, and warned that if he wanted to accuse us of wrongdoing, he would need something more reliable than his word and the poor English of a Korean teacher to back him up.

This particular incident seemed to change something in Angie. After seeing someone in authority step up for her, she got a lot more confident, and that confidence allowed her to redouble her efforts in class. Over the next several weeks, her grades improved, and she even went so far as to volunteer to be a student leader. "I want to be a real leader," she told us. "I won't put up with them using me to harass the students." From what I could see, she lived up to that conviction.

Unfortunately, my grades did not improve. I had two consecutive failures under my belt, and a big Listening exam in front of me on the day Kate went for her cryosurgery. The first sergeant had pulled me in to remind me that a Lack of Effort failure would be prosecutable, so I better do my best on this test; that did nothing to lessen the pressure.

I entered the room that day in a highly agitated state. This room wasn't our normal classroom, since we were taking an official proctored test; instead we were in a big room normally used for study hall on the first floor. It was designed for testing, so each desk had a tall, cloth-covered divider to reduce the likelihood of cheating. This design meant the acoustics in the room were terrible, and it didn't help that they were trying to play the test recording on an ancient cassette player at the front of the room. The volume was either too low, or distorted, with no middle ground. To top it all off, I was seated at the back of the stuffy room near an open window, and as I struggled to hear the muffled, muddled recording, the groundskeepers fired up the weed-eater right under my window.

The tests were graded on the spot, as we turned them in. I was not even allowed to return to the classroom. Instead, I went to the first sergeant's office, where I expected to be arrested and sent immediately to Fort Leavenworth.

"Well," she said, "I guess you did your best." I was not being arrested. In fact, I was going to be assigned night duty on Charge of Quarters until further notice while the Air Force decided my fate. I was to report that night for duty.

From there, I went home to await Kate's return from the doctor. Since she hadn't expected me to be at home, and we didn't yet have mobile phones in 1995, she had gone to the squadron first, so she had already heard my news. It was my turn to hear hers.

"The tests came back clean," she said. "There was no cancer... but they did find something unexpected." I braced myself, not knowing what to expect.

"I don't know how we managed it, but I'm a momma. Again."

12
Consequences

Kate and I were terrified.

The first pregnancy would have coincided with our class lengths in a way that would have allowed us to finish our schooling and, with any luck, get settled in at our first permanent duty station together with our newborn. There were some flaws in that plan, but now those flaws *were* the plan. With my fate in limbo, and Kate's final exams approaching, we had no idea where either of us would be when the baby arrived.

While I waited to learn what my new Air Force job would be, I was assigned to night CQ duty. "Charge of Quarters" is old school military talk for the 24/7 security and communications needs of the squadron. At a sleepy, nine-to-five school like DLI, this meant hourly walks around the campus with a flashlight to look for troublemakers and curfew violators, and weekends spent rounding up errant drunks who fell down hills or repentant lovers who managed to expose their intimacies to the poisoned oak growing in the woods around the grounds. (Yes, I once had to tend to the medical needs of an airman who had rolled through poisoned oak while naked. I do not recommend this if you are planning a date.)

After several tense weeks, I was told that because my aptitude scores at Basic Training were so high, and because other students had complained about our teachers during their exit interviews (I was not the first to wash out of that class), the decision had been made over Lt Col Gallegos's head to reassign me to another language. I was happy to learn that I was being placed in a Russian class, but that happiness and relief was tempered by the stress of the past seven months and the still-unanswered question of what would happen to Kate when she finished her classes in a couple of months.

Kate had problems of her own. As an Arabic student, and an outspoken Midwestern woman, she found herself constantly butting heads with her teaching team. They were already an interesting group, being an experiment in Arabic instruction. Where most Arabic classes were taught Modern Standard Arabic with an emphasis in one of the major regional dialects, taught by native speakers from that region, Kate's class was made up of speakers from all over the Arabic-speaking world. The head of the teaching team was a Saudi Muslim, and the others were an Iraqi, an Egyptian, a Saudi Christian, a Lebanese woman, and a U.S. Army Sergeant first class nicknamed "Bone Daddy."

They all hated each other.

The Korean culture is notorious for their fluid treatment of time, to the point that our Korean teachers told us early on that they were being watched by their superiors to ensure that they kept the Korean school running on a precise to-the-minute schedule. In contrast, Kate's Arabic class would lose entire 45-minute periods as the teaching team stood in the hallway arguing about who was supposed to be teaching in which room.

One day, when they did get around to entering the classroom, the teacher walked in, took one look at Kate, then turned on her heel and walked back out. A moment later, Bone Daddy called Kate to his office.

"Claudette says you disrespected her," he informed her, extending a formal Letter of Counseling for Kate to sign.

"How?" Kate asked, pushing the paper back at him. "I was sitting at my desk doing my homework."

"She says you showed her the bottom of your foot when she came into the room," he replied, silently insisting on getting her signature by including a pen when he slide the paper back.

"I had my legs crossed," Kate said, genuinely confused. "I'm wearing a skirt. You have to sit with your legs crossed when you're wearing a skirt."

She refused to sign, instead drawing a line through the signature block, writing, "I refuse to sign this statement," and signing that. It prompted a conversation back at the squadron with the first sergeant, who cautioned her to show proper respect to the teachers' cultures.

A few days later, a different teacher walked in, took one look at Kate, and then turned and walked back out. A moment later, Bone Daddy called Kate to his office.

"Dr. Asfour says you disrespected him," he informed her, extending a formal Letter of Counseling for Kate to sign.

"What now?" Kate asked in disgust. "I didn't have my legs crossed—I'm wearing combat boots today."

"He says you had your legs open when he came into the room. That's a very disrespectful way for a lady to sit."

"I'm not a lady," Kate said. "I'm an airman in the United States Air Force."

When this second LOC arrived at the squadron, Kate showed the first sergeant the two pieces of paper, and said simply, "They need to make up their minds." The first seargent crumpled both papers and tossed them out.

But the low-level harassment never stopped, and that, combined with the scattered and contradictory instruction that arose from having teachers of different dialects teaching and grading the students, meant that of the 40 students who began the course, only 12 made it to the final unit, including Kate. The Defense Language Proficiency Test served as the final exam, and scores on that test determined whether a student passed (with a Level 2 or higher) or failed. Only eight students passed. Kate was not one of these eight.

Kate had already been battling the bureaucracy over her obstetric care for our second pregnancy for months at that point. The rules stated that because her due date was seven months away, and her remaining class time was less than six months, she was not authorized to see a doctor off-base. Her first pregnancy had started when she still had nearly a year of class left so there had been no problem getting approval to see an obstetrician then, but now the best the on-base clinic could do was assign her to one of the field doctors who "had three kids of her own, so probably knew what she was doing."

She went to the first sergeant (the commander was TDY, of course) for help, but the first sergeant just shrugged helplessly. She went to the legal office, the inspector general, and called everyone they referred her to asking for help. Our situation wasn't a legal problem, because she wasn't being charged with a crime, and there was no wrongdoing to investigate, so no one could help her. Then she saw her final DLPT scores and realized that there were no good options left. Failing Arabic put her in the position I had been worried about when I failed Korean; she was likely to be reclassified and sent off to another tech school—unless she filed for a medical separation from the Air Force. She decided to take the discharge and try to get into the Reserves at some later date.

When the commander returned from her TDY, she saw my failure and reassignment and Kate's separation paperwork in her inbox, and determined that we had worked out some kind of conspiracy to trick the Air Force into giving us a free Arabic course. Again, I don't know what words were spoken, but after the pig, the draconian rules, the mistreatment of women *by* a woman, and the mishandling of nearly everything to do with our schooling, housing, and health, I suspect that a Kate with nothing to lose didn't hold back much.

Our relationship with the squadron was frosty after that, but they generally left us alone. Kate threw herself into the role of being a part-time office worker while she waited for her discharge to process, and I was finally able to focus on learning Russian.

My second language class had a lot in common with my first. There was the same general mix of 18-year-old Army kids, older-but-no-wiser airmen, and a smattering of Navy and Marines. There was a sense of *deja-vu* in the first weeks, as the weak were culled from the rest of the herd, but the Russian teachers seemed to know what they were doing, and they were able to identify the students who wouldn't be able to make the final cut early and put together tests that would wash out those students in the first couple of months, leaving the rest of the course to nurture and develop those who were serious about being there.

This might have been my Air Force bias showing, but it seemed like mostly Army kids who washed out first. There were a few, like my friends Brent and Todd, who were interested in language and clearly wanted to learn; but half of that class was made up of dazed, clueless kids from the middle of nowhere who were shocked to have made it through Army Basic. One of these guys had trouble sleeping at night— partly due to the partying and mayhem of life in the Army barracks, but mainly due to the stress—and he would doze through classes all day. This meant he struggled harder with homework, which meant poor sleep, and a vicious cycle. He actually went to the clinic to complain about the tension headaches, and they prescribed codeine, of all things, because of course you want to supply an 18-year-old kid with narcotics when they are stressed out and falling behind in an intensive language course.

It's hard to overstate how refreshing it was to deal with the Russian teachers after the horror show of being in the Korean and Arabic schools. For one thing, in contrast to the Korean commitment to the fiction that a teacher is superior in all ways to any student, our homeroom teacher, Alla Vladimirovna, entered the room on day one, saying:

"I wish to apologize for my poor fluency in English. I just returned from a year-long immersion training course with the NASA astronauts who will be stationed on the Mir space station, and I was not allowed to practice my English as I normally would. Perhaps if you help me brush up on my language, it will even help you understand Russian better, no?"

Compare that to "Ris-ten to tay-puh, and-uh repeat-uh," and tell me that either of those two teachers is at Level 2.

We loved Alla, and Mr. Janowsky, who was a Polish speaker teaching his *third* language to speakers of his *fifth* language. We loved the irascible Lev Millman, who looked like he had been upholstered in brown tweed, and the gregarious Ilya Leavit, who each managed to teach us to swear without breaking the rules against doing so. They weren't perfect people, and we suffered from as much culture clash as any class, but they genuinely respected us, which made working with them a lot easier.

As Kate's Air Force career drew to an end, she spent more time at the Russian Village complex, either picking me up after school or having lunch with me and my classmates. She and her swelling abdomen became celebrities in our class, with the mysterious baby showing up in our homework assignments and conversation hours as the teachers would ask me about "vash rebyonok"—*your baby*. My classmates preferred to refer to it as "vash plod"—the Russian word for *fetus*, to the great chagrin and displeasure of the teachers.

Most of my memories of this time seem distant and secondhand now. I remember hearing about the kinds of adventures that my classmates were having but not really participating. They had their bachelor party incidents, and their drunks, but I wasn't in the middle of that stuff anymore. I missed out when the company commander pulled a surprise inspection on a Friday evening, when half of the students were already three sheets to the wind, and someone on the third floor decided to try to poop over the balcony. I wasn't around when a group of Marines got into a fight with some local drug dealers on the beach below Cannery Row, resulting in a public fight between the post commandant and the mayor of Seaside, who complained about the number of his citizens those Marines sent to the hospital.

But I was there when Brent improvised a glorious 45-minute tale in Russian during conversation hour in which he organized a terrorist cell at a restaurant called The Happy Camel and concocted three successively unlikely scenarios involving exploding hamsters, a skateboard joust, and a bathroom duel between Mr. Millman and Mr.

Janowsky. I remember thinking that either we were all Level 2 that day, or Kenny Lee's theory about humor was bullshit.

Brent's facility with the dictionary was unparalleled. One day in class, the Army guys conspired to play a joke which involved each of them raising their hand and asking to go to the bathroom.

"Yes," said Mr. Millman.

"*Mozhno mne poidu v tualet?*" asked the first private.

"Yes," said Mr. Millman. The first private returned, and the next raised a hand.

"Yes," said Mr. Millman.

"*Mozhno mne poidu v tualet?*" asked the second private.

"Yes, go," said Mr. Millman, annoyed. The second returned a third raised his hand, but Mr. Millman was onto them, now. "No!" he shouted. "No more *v tualet*! *Nelzya vam v tualet!* The next person to ask to go to the toilet, will be executed by the Secret Police!"

Hearing this, Brent frantically flipped through his dictionary for a few minutes, then raised his hand.

Mr. Millman eyed him suspiciously. "Are you going to ask to go *v tualet*?" he asked.

"No," Brent said, innocently. "*Ya dolzhen otvodit yasheritsu.*"

Mr. Millman looked puzzled. "You have to ...drain... a lizard? What does..." The lightbulb flicked on, and he made a disgusted face. "Oh, just go, already!"

But without a doubt, the best part about being there was the birth of our daughter. We named her Cambria after the little seaside artists' village we discovered on a trip down the Pacific Coast Highway, and she became the center of our world.

Babies are not known for respecting schedules, but ours came courteously during a break between our various final exams. We had just enough time to learn how to take care of her, and show her off to all of our friends, and then class was over. I had passed, and after nearly two years in Monterey, it was time to move on.

And so, without really knowing what we were getting into, we packed our belongings, and left—together, and with our healthy and beautiful baby.

13

United Queendom

I made a circuit of the large room, bearing a tray full of steaming mugs.

"Ta, mate," came the usual response, as my British colleague collected his beverage of choice. Sometimes that beverage was "coffee, NATO," which meant black with two sugars; most often they simply ordered tea. It had taken me a while to learn the subtle and unwritten rules about making tea for the British, but by this point in my career, I felt rather accomplished at the task.

Lee took a sip, and gasped theatrically. "What the hell did you do to that tea?" he shouted. "It's still boiling!"

"I boiled it," I replied, blandly.

My ability to display this kind of dry, deadpan humor was considered a rare trait for an American abroad, and it had won me a number of cool points with my British counterparts. Not a large number, but a number. I still had to suffer myriad small indignities, such as the day I pedaled my bicycle up the quarter-mile road from our house to the work building, and one of my shift mates slowed his car as he passed to shout, "Pedal faster, ya fat necky Yank spam twat!" ("Spam" was a holdover nickname for Americans from World War II, meaning "specially processed American meat.") I didn't really mind that kind of treatment, though, as it was generally a sign of acceptance.

I felt lucky to have been accepted at all, considering the way my presence had been thrust into the middle of a Royal Air Force work center by the USAF. After leaving Monterey, spending 19 more weeks of training in Texas and a year in Maryland, I had been sent to the United Kingdom where I was the lowest ranking person in a tiny detachment. Even though I was junior by any nation's standard, the USAF had insisted on assigning me to a position that the RAF usually reserved for their senior technical experts. I hadn't been very well trained, in my own opinion, but I learned quickly and showed enough humility and humor about my place in the world that my RAF co-workers could tolerate the situation.

Others did not fare so well in adjusting to the very different culture. A technical sergeant who had arrived on station the day after I had proved not to be very knowledgeable or adaptable at all. The RAF watch officers wisely tested him and refused to let him join their 24/7 watch rotation, as he couldn't handle any of the systems they used and persistently made simple mistakes that tended to cause embarrassing fallout. The whole three years I was there, he answered telephones with the name of his previous duty station in Colorado. When the USAF promoted him to master sergeant (full disclosure: he was apparently great at multiple choice tests), the RAF sergeants created a new "job" for him on the day watch as an "Environmental Awareness Analyst." He was supposed to review the daily newspapers looking for articles related to our mission, but then he turned in his first report to the group captain. The group captain is a Royal Air Force rank somewhat equivalent to a colonel or U.S. Navy captain, and our MSgt gave him what amounted to a blog post worthy of the worst of the right-wing fever swamps, copying a paragraph about the U.S. bombing of a Sudanese aspirin factory and then adding his low opinion of President Clinton's morals in all caps.

He spent the rest of his tour in our USAF admin office running errands and managing annual training.

Just as I was beginning to feel comfortable working on my own without worrying that I was going to cause an international incident, I was informed that our unit would be gaining another tech sergeant; she would be my trainee at first, since she had never worked our exact mission before, and once trained, she would become my supervisor.

Expressing my discomfort with this situation did no good then, so I won't bother recounting it now.

Her name was Sally, and she arrived on a mid-watch. After introducing her around to the key personnel on the watch floor, I tried to dive straight into learning the equipment. Introductions were easy, as most of our colleagues were named either Dave or Steve. There were at least five Daves in our work center, and three American Steves plus a few British ones scattered around through other parts of the building. The British RAF and Army enlisted gents—and they were mostly gents—favored Neil and Lofty, the latter of which is a common nickname for British airmen. But rather than talk about the job, Sally had a lot of questions that she did not realize were very awkward for me.

"I heard these Brits aren't very politically correct," she said in what seemed to me to be a very loud voice. "These guys all seem nice enough, though." She clearly couldn't see that her monologue was being heard by our neighbors, who grinned at me evilly from behind her, and began making obscene gestures suggestive of possible training techniques. "I'm surprised there aren't more women working here," she announced, unaware that I had made a similar comment on my first night, only to be treated to a spectacularly anti-feminist explanation of a woman's proper role in the Forces. She was spared that performance, but our gesticulating neighbor excused himself from the room with an apparent choking fit.

My discomfort was threefold. First, I wanted to make a decent impression on the person who would be writing my annual evaluation. Second, the Brits were all too familiar with our then-recent Equal Employment Opportunity policies in the U.S. armed forces that forbade any kind of inappropriate conversation, and they thrived on the entertainment value of drawing me into inappropriate situations in front of my U.S. bosses. For them, this was all part of the wind up. Third, I was forming an unpleasant first impression of Sally and didn't entirely trust myself to avoid blowing that first impression on this first night.

We managed to get Sally logged into her workstation, and I walked her through the basics; open this program, set these control windows, minimize these icons for later... She seemed to be getting the swing of things. I turned to my own workstation and donned my headphones to start catching up on my work for the night, but Sally tapped my shoulder. "It's not working," she shouted, not realizing that her own headphones were still on.

I tried to troubleshoot her problem for a few minutes, but none of the program windows would display. I kept asking her, "Did you put the icons I showed you on the desktop?" She affirmed that she had, but I had no success figuring out what was wrong, and I ended up rebooting her workstation, a process which took about 10 minutes.

When I restored her workstation again and turned back around, she soon tapped my shoulder again. Same problem. We went through this two or three times, and I realized that instead of minimizing her windows and arranging the icons like I kept showing her, she was sliding whole windows off the screen, where they could no longer be accessed with the mouse or keyboard. I was re-explaining what icons were for a third time when two of our shift's Army sergeants walked over to introduce themselves.

"How's it going, Sally?" said Tommy. Tommy was a cute, tiny Scotsman with the kind of smile that belongs on a television game show. He stood just behind her left shoulder, while Tommo, a squat, tough squaddie from Liverpool stood over to her right. She couldn't turn to see both of them at the same time, and when she turned to answer Tommy, Tommo caught my eye, and began pointed from Sally to me with one hand while simulating felatio with the other.

"It's going okay," Sally said to Tommy, who grinned like this was the best news since V-E Day. Then she turned so she could tell Tommo, "I don't know if Tad's a very good teacher, though!" Tommo looked deeply sympathetic and thoughtful while Tommy, now out of Sally's line of sight, began furiously air-humping the back of her head.

Tommo drew her out, asking what made me a bad teacher. I concentrated on keeping my face blank as Tommy's fists pumped like pistons past his thrusting pelvis and he bit his lower lip. "Oh, I just don't know why he keeps bringing religion up," Sally was saying. "He keeps making fun of Catholic icons for some reason."

Tommy composed himself quickly and leaned into her field of view to tap at her workstation. Tommo took his turn again, this time flicking his tongue obscenely through his forked fingers and goggling his eyes. "Well, you see, Sally, these wee pictures are the 'icons' that tell you which program they represent. If you click that box there, they sit along the side of the screen where you can reach them."

"Oh, great!" Sally gushed. "Now I get it!" Tommy and Tommo beamed at her and bade her a good night and strolled to their side of the room.

"Alright, mate?" Tommy asked me, leering. I nodded. "Why don't you pop the kettle on while Sally does her work, then?"

It was a welcome suggestion, but I gave him the bird for the sake of my own dignity, and both of them laughed as I headed for the tiny kitchen.

*

My work schedule alternated between two 12-hour mid shifts (from 7 p.m. to 7 a.m.) and two 12-hour day shifts (from 7 a.m. to 7 p.m.), with a "sleep day" in between. This was great, in a way, because even though we technically ended up working 48 hours per week, we got three days off every week. Kate and I were able to spend that time seeking out adventure with our precocious baby daughter.

Bria was not quite two years old when we arrived in the summer of 1998. Teletubbies were on the telly, as was the FIFA World Cup. Cher was sitting at number one on the charts with her hit single, "Life After Love" so we got to hear that every day on the radio, until it was usurped by South Park's Chef singing "Chocolate Salty Balls."

We tooled around the countryside in a red Mini Cooper that we really couldn't afford, learning the disappointment of visiting National Heritage sites: after two hours on tiny country roads that wound through farmlands—called fen roads—with a bored toddler, the only thing to see was an empty field. Sometimes we found a plaque describing whatever had once stood there, if we were lucky. We did enjoy living under the practice airspace of the Red Arrows, the demonstration flight based at nearby RAF Waddington, and we loved the Christmas Fair in Lincoln.

But there were a lot of challenges for us. Our detachment was a good two-hour drive from the American bases at RAF Mildenhall and RAF Lakenheath, where the nearest Base Exchange, or BX, and commissary were located. Our squadron personnel flight and medical services were on Mildenhall, but our dentists were on RAF Alconbury—another 45-minute drive. And when Kate found out she was pregnant again, we had to decide whether she was more comfortable visiting an obstetrician at Mildenhall or finding a British doctor closer to our house in Lincolnshire.

After an appointment with the local NHS doctor, in which he took her temperature with a nubbly thermometer (hand-washed under the tap with room temperature water after taking her reading and replaced on the shelf where he had found it) and recommended a pint of Guinness each week (for the iron), Kate opted for a third choice: she arranged to return to Omaha, Nebraska with Bria, stay with her parents for the third trimester, and have the baby there. I would save up my leave, and join her for the birth, then bring the three of them back to England.

This plan worked well enough except for the fact that I didn't like being apart from Kate and Bria for so long. We talked on the phone almost every night, but with my rotating schedule and my life-long inability to understand time zones, we were rarely at our best for these calls. For her part, Kate would vent about the ways her mother was driving her crazy, and I would moan about missing them.

You might think I would live the rowdy life of the bachelor while I had the chance, but that has never been my strength. I did go out drinking one night with Lee and Neil, which was good, but after four Red Bulls with vodka, the Marilyn Monroe and Michael Jackson impersonators, and a game that started out as billiards and ended as darts, I decided to stick with coffee and this new internet service called Netflix for my entertainment needs.

I did attend a British "barbecue" one afternoon. This involved beer, of course, and someone putting frozen cuts of meat on a charcoal grill next to a pot of Heinz Tomato Soup, lighting the charcoal, and eventually plopping the thawed meat into the soup to boil until we were drunk enough to eat it. I attempted to put Stevie Ray Vaughan in the CD player to bring some authenticity to at least one aspect of the event, but Tommo declared that to be "slit yer throat music," and demanded some real music, like George Michael's greatest hits.

At last, the day came for me to start my 45 days of leave in Omaha. Once I arrived, there was little for me to do besides watch old Star Trek Voyager episodes with Bria and try to avoid the angst and drama in the house as Kate and her mother demonstrated why Kate had left home so enthusiastically at eighteen.

When the birthday finally arrived, we were thrilled to find ourselves with a little boy, and we had a sturdy Irish name picked out for him. Aside from a traumatic occasion when little Séamus managed to poop into his mommy's eye, his arrival brought joy to us all.

After getting an expedited passport for our new son, we returned to the UK. We almost lost him, carrier and all, to a violent updraft while changing planes in Iceland. The wind from the frosty fields whipped across the tarmac and threatened to carry off his car seat, but we made it.

We arrived at the onset of autumn, and for a while things seemed to go back to something that seemed normal. But normal meant odd hours, weeks without sunlight, and a nearly constant grey drizzle falling out of the sky. It wasn't long before normal turned into something darker.

Looking back, I wonder if we weren't suffering from actual diagnosable conditions. Postpartum Depression was Kate's biggest fear, but when we talked to our closest friends about how we were feeling, they admitted to experiencing some of the same feelings. We figured PPD wouldn't affect multiple families, so maybe the mental anguish was just normal for new parents. We'd also read about Seasonal Affective Disorder in magazines and on the internet, but none of us was sure that was even a real thing, and none of us wanted to deal with the stigma of asking the military doctors about a possible career-limiting mental illness.

And so, everyone decided to muddle along. Our detachment commander was a young captain with his first command, and while he tried to understand and help, but he was really out of his depth. He was one of those people who pretended to listen, but suffered from selective hearing; then he would become embarrassed and suspicious when he discovered he was in the wrong.

For example, when I first arrived on base, and he had asked me to bring him all of my receipts to see what kinds of expenses were involved for a junior enlisted person to transfer to this assignment. In theory, the Air Force pays for everything when someone is ordered to make a Permanent Change of Station, or PCS. But after accounting for the extra time we spent in the hotel waiting for housing to open up, and the rental car I was told (but not officially "ordered" on my paper orders) to rent, and the deposit to rent the house we ended up in, and myriad other expenses that weren't covered in the flat reimbursement the Air Force gave me, I turned in a report that said I was $1,500 in debt because of my family's move.

"What?" The captain shoved away my copies and receipts in disbelief. "I can't accept this!" For all his protests, and his refusal to give my numbers to our squadron commander, I did notice the Air Force Times headline later that month that said, "Average E-4 Accrues $1,500 Debt for a PCS." And I noticed that he never mentioned questioning my integrity.

Over the course of my tour he did insist, despite my increasingly firm objections, that I should consider re-enlisting. This was a decision that I had not really made until giving this England assignment a chance, but after misadventure upon bureaucratic misadventure—"training" Sally, the $1,500 debt from our PCS, the stupid hoops we had to jump through to get "guaranteed" support—I was not inclined to spend more time in the service than I already had. Of course, "I'm still thinking about it," was never the answer that any of my Air Force superiors wanted to hear. The captain, along with every other career service member I crossed paths with, seemed intent on turning me gung ho with talk of the pension, the benefits, and how good I had it!

What the captain failed to appreciate was the way those little indignities added up. Every month for six months after my return from our trip to Omaha, I got tapped for a random drug test. I didn't really mind, since these had to be done at RAF Alconbury, and I got to file a $45 voucher for local area travel. I figured since I was in England for 36 months, that was their way of repaying me for the $1,500 PCS debt.

One of the dust-ups we had with the captain had to do with his email signature. We were all required to have an official USAF email account, and we had to check that email at the detachment office on a regular basis. The captain would send us announcements about things like annual training requirements, TDY opportunities, the aforementioned drug tests, and other USAF business. But while he frequently lectured us about the policy requiring a signature block, and the policy about not having "inappropriate quotes" in them, his signature block signed off every email with the following:

IN NOMINE DOMINE JESU CHRISTE.

Steve had pointed out to him that this was an inappropriate quote to include in an official email signature block, and the captain had insisted that it was not. They went round and round about the First Amendment, freedom of expression versus the Establishment Clause, until I pointed out that the captain was ordering me to pee in a cup "in the name of Jesus Christ." He changed his sig block, and we never mentioned the question of his integrity.

Even when the drug tests eventually petered out, there was other routine squadron business that came up. One month, I got summoned down for "CJR paperwork." I didn't know what that was, but I traveled down to the squadron, found the office that processed the CJR, and I learned that a CJR was a "career job reservation," which meant that if I decided to re-enlist, I would have a billet reserved. I read it carefully, and since it specifically said signing the document did not re-enlist me, I signed it.

The next month, I got another notice to go down and sign a CJR. The Captain asked why I hadn't gone down the previous month, when he told me to. I said I did, and he had signed the travel voucher to prove it. He grumbled, but did not acknowledge that he was once again questioning my integrity. I went down, signed the CJR, came back, and collected another $45.

It happened again the next month. This time, when I went to the office where they collected these, I asked, "What do I need to do to stop getting these requests? My captain thinks I'm not completing them."

"Well," the personnel sergeant shrugged. "If you decline to test for promotion, you won't be eligible to re-enlist."

"Great! Let me do that!"

"What? But that will end your career!" he gasped.

"I know. Weird how I would want that, isn't it?"

The closest I came to reconsidering and even entertaining the idea of re-enlisting was during the military ball that year, when I was seated next to a chief master sergeant who had been a Russian linguist when he started out. He asked me about my plans, and I braced myself for the usual lecture about what a fool I was to give up All of This… but he just nodded and said, "Well, I just want to thank you for your service. The fact that you enlisted at all is more than most of your peers have done for the country." My Air Force blue heart swelled two sizes that day, but it didn't change my mind.

And so, when the captain found out that I had thrown away my promising future as a cup-filling soldier of Christ, he pretty much stopped talking to me.

At least he wasn't questioning my integrity.

But my growing family and I found ways to spend quality time together, and with our friends. We played cards with Randy and Kim, and watched movies with Steve and Geana. We managed to plan a train trip to France, and visited Euro-Disney (don't judge, the kids loved it!), and my parents visited on my birthday for a car trip to Scotland. There were happy times and bright spots, but we were looking forward to going back to the States.

One night, as I wandered outside at 7 p.m., at the end of a long day watch, I noticed a familiar car speeding up the main road. Kate had been down to Mildenhall for a medical checkup, for her and the baby, and I hadn't expected her back so soon. But here she was, pulling into the parking lot, and crying. I climbed into the car and asked what was wrong; baby Séamus and Bria seemed alright, asleep in their car seats.

"I'm pregnant," she said. "And the baby is due the month you get out of the Air Force."

She was sobbing, clearly terrified. I knew why. I had no job lined up, no idea what we were going to do when I got out. None of the programs for hiring veterans seemed to have any information that applied to me, and none of the jobs I was applying for online were panning out. She wasn't wrong to be scared or upset.

But I put my finger under her chin, and tilted her head to look at me. "Sweetheart," I said, with an uncontrollable joy creeping up from my toes and into my eyes, "that is awesome news!"

14
Flashbacks:
Five Midnight Vignettes

Midnight. Texas. 1996.

My classmates and I formed up at the track for a midnight PT session.

My training class was scheduled for a week of swing shift to simulate what shift work would be like once we graduated. Kate was trying to match my shift schedule, she said, so she had brought baby Bria and our dog to the track. After two years at DLI, surrounded by everyone in our squadron, she was having trouble adjusting to being at home all day without any other adults around, and she enjoyed seeing the familiar faces of people from my class.

The trip from DLI to Texas for the follow-on training had been a leap into the dark for us. Despite the lectures about all of the couples who were married at DLI and divorced at Goodfellow, the staff seemed curiously clueless about the rules for me taking my family with me. None of the funding we were told to expect panned out, so we only learned after we arrived that we couldn't afford the off-base apartment we were renting. The unit seemed miffed that I had not simply left Kate and Bria in California, but after the round of base closures that year, Fort Ord had been designated an "open base," and there had been problems with homeless people and drug dealers from neighboring Seaside breaking into the houses. I wasn't about to leave my wife and newborn behind for six months while I muddled through training, so here we were.

Our student leaders seemed like infants to us. Those of us who had gone through year-long language classes at DLI had at least a year in service (I had two, thanks to my failed Korean course), and these kids were fresh out of Basic. Some of them were from the firefighter school, and some were linguists like us but had tested high enough to skip DLI. We thought that was admirable, having just acquired an appreciation for people who were bilingual; but these folks had been told that we would look down on them for not having our year of schooling, and they mostly treated us with open contempt.

Midnight PT was our choice; the other option would have been to come in before class started at 1500, and really, no one wanted to run before an afternoon class. We did not care for the overbearing staff or our obnoxious fellow students, but after midnight, we had the base to ourselves. No firedogs razzing us for being egghead linguists; no frustrated student leaders trying to enforce obscure regulations (What do you mean I have to carry a flashlight at all times? My car is *right there*!); and there were no officers around to remember to salute when scampering across base. It was much more fun this way, especially since my classmates got a chance to coo over our baby; and Maloney, the great Irish linebacker from Kate's hometown of Omaha, got a chance to run with our overweight dog.

Of course, the lights were on a timer, and they shut off in the middle of our lap. Everyone went silent and froze where they were on the track. I couldn't resist yelling, "Oh, *no*! I'm not safe, because I'm not carrying my regulation flashlight!"

"Shut up, Callin!"

*

Midnight. Maryland. 1997.

Kate was 21 years old, and she had the buzz on to prove it. We sent Bria to stay with a responsible friend, and had all of the others over to enjoy beers and Jello shooters. She made several varieties, with different kinds of Jello, and there were dozens of them.

"I'm gonna go see why Jack and Shari aren't here yet," she hiccupped, picking up a plate with a selection of treats. I followed to make sure she didn't fall down on her way to our neighbor's house. We were both concerned that they hadn't arrived yet.

Before we got to their driveway, they came bursting out the front door. Jack was in a wheelchair; he was paralyzed from the waist down after a motorcycle accident a year and a half earlier. Shari was in the Navy, and Jack was former Army. They were usually a lot of fun to be around and always seemed happy. Not tonight. They were screaming at each other, and taking swings at each other, trying to punch each other to punctuate their insults.

Jack caught Shari by the hair and pulled her down over the arm of his chair, yanking her head around with his powerful arms. She screamed desperately and flailed with her legs, trying to push away from him.

Kate just stood there gaping for a moment, struggling to snap out of the champagne fog and take action. Someone found a phone. Before we knew it, the police were there.

An officer escorted Kate back into our house to take her statement and to ask if anyone from our party had seen anything. All of us sat uncomfortably around the living room, looking from the assorted bottles to the officer, and thinking about our recent experiences at DLI with alcohol and authority figures.

"Quite a pawty," said the second officer. Eyes darted, and feet shuffled. He pointed at me. "Aw you the miwitawy member?" he asked. Somehow, all movement in the room froze as I nodded. We had all been conditioned by our time at DLI to fear authority in conjunction with intoxication, and it was clear from the faces around the room that this fear was warring with an immature, alcohol-fueled mirth. No one wanted to be That Guy.

"And who is the witness?" he asked.

"Me!" Kate chirped. "I'm finally 21!"

"That's gweat ma'am," he said, "So teww me what you saw…"

*

Midnight. Russia. 1999.

Regular language refresher training was a requirement for every linguist, and since I was stationed in Europe, I was selected for the six-week Russian refresher course at the George Marshall Foreign Language Training Center, Europe. I had enjoyed the first five weeks in Germany immensely. Garmisch-Partenkirchen is absolutely beautiful in June. I bought a bicycle at the tiny American exchange and toured the countryside; I climbed an Alp, the Kramerspitz, with my friend Brady; I bought a train ticket and made my way across the country to visit Brent, who was stationed near Wuerzburg. But now I was in Saint Petersburg, Russia for the final week. This was considered the ultimate in language immersion.

I looked out the window of my room in the Hotel Neva, watching the sunset. The sun had been setting for nearly an hour, and it was as dark as it was going to get that night. By 0030, it would be sunrise. I could hear singing and fireworks down at one of the drawbridges. I knew my friends were out there, enjoying the party, but I was sick. Whether it was the 15 ounce *stokan* of vodka, or the steady diet of sausages, or the tiny bit of municipal water I had allowed to get in my mouth (we were warned that the water in the pipes came from, and returned to, the river) it didn't matter. I was tied to my room until this awfulness passed from me.

For that one night, I was trapped watching MTV-Rossiya. I sat amazed as Beavis and Butthead were overdubbed live, apparently by one disinterested man with a microphone, who grew less disinterested as he got into the show and finished the program doing both character voices and chuckling at the jokes. ("Nu, kakaya zadnitsa! Huh, huh!") I ended the evening with a bizarre music video countdown including Metallica's cover of "Whiskey In the Jar," followed by what looked like Doc Severinsen and his twin chasing the Fresh Prince around a czar's palace; then a caustic Russian metal band playing their instruments while covered in either oatmeal or cement, and rounding out the Top Ten with the inevitable Cher (I no longer believe in life after love, Cher). This was horrible, but the rest of the trip was amazing.

A couple of my classmates and I went to the Bolshoi Ballet, we visited the Hermitage museum, we shopped at Dom Knigi, and we rode the Metro—not because we needed to go anywhere, but because the teachers felt we needed to ride down the quarter-mile escalator into the most opulent train station most of us will ever see. I also found a CD store and discovered the exchange rate (24 rubles to the dollar) allowed me to buy more music than I could possibly carry back in my luggage. I spent $10 for 20 discs and then realized that I had just dropped about three months of the average Russian's salary on *The Best of Falco* and *Radiohead World Music 200% Ultra Hits*, featuring their hit single, "Greep." I felt like an asshole.

My roommate, Eric, had a great time. He was far more fluent in Russian than I was, and as an African-American, he attracted the attention of every child in the city. I watched transfixed as he fielded questions from a group of thirty 10-year-olds in flawless Russian. "No, I didn't catch fire—this is my skin. If I want to get lighter, I go lay out under a full moon." They adored him.

Katya was our main instructor. She and Eric and I all had little daughters about the same age, so we had a lot of fun improvising conversations about our kids. When she asked, "How do you punish your child?" I couldn't think of a way to communicate a "time-out" so I said, "Ya yeyo razbit v zhopu," which does *not* translate as "I smack her on the bottom."

Katya reddened, explained that I had just announced that I "punch her up the ass," and then taught us the words *shlopat* (to spank) and *zadnitsa* (butt, as in "Nu, kakaya zadnitsa!" or "Hey, nice butt!").

"You should not spank, though," she cautioned. "It is better to give time-out."

*

Midnight. Lincolnshire. 2000.

We had waited for Y2K, half-believing that something momentous would happen, but the world did not end.

Kate and I sprawled outside, in Kim and Randy's front yard, drunk out of our goddamned minds.

Kim and Randy were big fans of Bria, but had insisted that they were not cut out for parenting. Bria was one of a kind, so what were their chances of making a kid as cool as her? Then, when they met Séamus, they thought, okay, we need one of these.

Kate and I were laying in the yard, looking up at the sky. The weather seemed warm for January, but that might just have been the tequila.

"This is beautiful," she said. I agreed. "I still don't like it here," she continued. "Why is that?" I didn't know. "I should be happy, but I just want to go home."

I held her hand, and wanted to be home with her. Then I realized it wasn't the alcohol making me feel warm, and I kissed her.

"Why did you do that?" she demanded.

"Happy New Year."

*

Midnight. London. 2001.We were almost free.

Baby Lars had been born without any disasters befalling us on the long road from our house to the hospital at RAF Lakenheath. He came out with an audible *pop* and had the cord around his neck. This was no problem for the doctor, but it was the one thing I had feared about the possibility of giving birth on the side of the road. Now our boy was here, squalling lustily, and weighing nearly three times as much as the other babies born that night.

We hadn't had the leave or the money to pull another trip to the States, so Lars would be the only baby of ours born outside the United States. We had worried until the last minute that his passport wouldn't come through in time and that we would be stuck in the UK.

Kate, Bria, Séamus and Lars were asleep in the temporary housing accommodations, and I was outside, looking nervously at the sky, thinking about my last conversation with the captain.

The captain had actually left before the end of my tour by four months, but before he left, he asked me again why I had decided not to reenlist. I asked him if he was familiar with the story of Jacob and Rachel, from the Bible.

In that story, Jacob fell in love with Rachel, and asked her father Laban if he could marry her. Laban said he could if Jacob first indentured himself to Laban for seven years. Jacob agreed, and after he finished his seven years, Laban threw a grand wedding feast. When Jacob woke up the next morning though, he found that the girl under the wedding veil was Rachel's older sister, Leah.

"I thought you knew," Laban told him. "It's our custom to marry off the older daughter first. If you want to marry Rachel, you need to indenture yourself to me for another seven years."

Jacob agreed, and after seven years, he got to marry Rachel.

"I've been in the Air Force for my seven years, Captain," I told him. "This isn't the bitch I wanted to marry, and I don't intend to get suckered into another seven years."

I had been pretty pleased with myself at the time for provoking the look of shock and distaste on his face. After the captain left, and had been replaced by a new commander, and after I had gone through the rather lame series of résumé-writing classes and "job fairs" known as Transition Assistance & Planning, I had to face a hard reality. I kept focusing on being excited about going home. I told myself that some job prospect would come up. I ignored the fact that I was taking my family straight back into the situation I thought I had left behind when I enlisted: unemployed, living in my parent's house, and clueless about what to do next.

In the weeks leading up to our departure date, I had been having a recurring dream. In the dream, I was in my service dress uniform, standing at Gatwick Airport with my family and all our baggage, ready to fly away from England and the Air Force for good. I looked up, and I saw Russian bombers flying in ordered patterns overhead, dropping bombs on the airstrip so that we couldn't leave.

In the dream, I was screaming at them, "No! You bastards! Noooo! I can't stay here anymore!"

I woke up in a panic in the Air Force temporary housing quarters where my family slept, waiting for our flight—leaving out of Heathrow, not Gatwick, stupid dream—and I went outside to watch the sky. Our flight was not taking off for another five hours. But we were almost free.

It was summer of 2001. What could go wrong?

Part III:
Fatherhood

Still Life, With Beard

1

On the Road: Driving Man, Part 1

I sat in the drivers' waiting area, duffel bag on the floor beside me, waiting for my Driver/Trainer to arrive. All I had was a name on a piece of paper: "Thomas Martinez (non-smoking)." Every time a driver entered the room, I looked up, wondering if it was him. I had no idea what to expect.

I had an image of spending these next four weeks on the road with the lead singer of Los Lobos, probably because my instructor for the last 18 weeks of truck driving school had looked like him. Al Munoz was a New York Puerto Rican who had ended up in Phoenix teaching guys like me how to drive trucks because driving trucks for 25 years had left him medically incapable of doing much else.

Seemed all of the instructors had been "rode hard and put away wet" as they said; they all had gum or suckers on hand because they were all trying to quit smoking. A few were diabetic, and one—the "old guy"—who looked like he was 80 based on his decrepit appearance and obvious medical frailties, shocked us all by telling us he was only 58. "Bennies did this to me!" he would crow. Benzedrine was the first pharmaceutical amphetamine, and had been popular with truckers in the 1970s to keep them awake for racking up extra miles (and thus, extra pay).

The company I was joining seemed like a nice outfit. They were one of the newer fleets, based in the Southwest, and their building was new and clean, like a comfortably scaled-down version of a car showroom. Our instructors had spoken highly of this company, though none of them had driven for them. The teachers had mainly driven for the bigger, older firms, like Swift, which they had mocked for being shady and hiring "anyone with a stick." I looked around, hoping I would fit in once I got the hang of things.

But in the middle of my pondering, a squat white guy with a Marine Corps bottle cap-style camouflage hat came out and called my name. I stood up, and he sized me up with a blank expression.

"You got your gear?" he asked. I nodded. "Good. I'm Tom. Come on, then."

I followed him out of the terminal, chiding myself for making assumptions. I grew up in Arizona, so I should know better than to stereotype a surname. We went out to his truck, and stashed my duffel in a big compartment under the lower bunk. "I've gotta get some paperwork and crap. There's a spray bottle and rag in there, so just clean up the truck while I'm doing that. This is your home for the next month, so get used to cleaning up after yourself."

He strode off back toward the terminal and left me there holding the spray bottle. I suppose I could have gotten upset about it and made a big fuss, but judging by his hat and the USMC seal in the corner of the window, I guessed what he was up to, so I cleaned the hell out of that truck.

He came back after nearly an hour, surveyed the truck, nodded at me with approval, and climbed aboard.

*

I woke up slowly, tempted to let the motion of the truck rock me back to sleep, but I sensed that I was probably expected to get up at this point. I pulled on my jeans, rolled up my sleeping bag, and slipped into the passenger seat. The morning was glorious, and we were heading west toward Barstow, California; the desert scrub spreading in every direction, the sky stretching and arching its back like a cat, on tip-toes at the horizon, so pale a shade of blue that it was almost black again.

"This is why I wanted to do this," I said, indicating the landscape. I had told him all about England; the long nights and days stuck on the watch floor, the dreary days and nights spent huddled in our little house, hoping we would be able to handle the bills for another month on a junior enlisted man's salary. And how, after 9/11, I was thinking of going back to it. Probably would, if this job didn't work out.

"You're doing fine," he would lie. He'd given up the drill sergeant role, now that he trusted me. Washing his truck with no complaining had almost completely won him over. He kept telling me the mistakes I made were small. "It's a *forgivable* mistake, as long as it can be repaired and no one was hurt," he would say. But more and more I was starting to dread being on the road in a truck by myself. The things that had gone wrong—leaving the paperwork with the wrong trailer at the swap-yard in Calexico; getting lost in Los Angeles; climbing Mt. Shasta during a blizzard—these things had terrified me in ways that I didn't think were healthy.

Worse, I still couldn't handle backing the truck. I had passed the test to gain my Commercial Driver's License (CDL), but I could tell it was a close thing. I couldn't see the tires in the mirror at night, couldn't hook up a trailer by myself, and certainly couldn't back up to a loading dock. What good was a driver if all he could handle was the driving part?

I didn't trust myself to objectively gauge how well I was doing, though. Tom had purposely created a lot of pressure on me during all of those situations, trying to see how I would handle it. He'd kept us on the road without stopping for the first two days straight, waiting to see when I would ask to eat or shower or go to the bathroom. I spent those two days wondering when this crazy ex-Marine would ever stop to eat, shower, or use the bathroom! Fortunately, the truck needed to eat every 600 miles or so, so I had a daily opportunity to perform my necessary.

But we still hadn't eaten. When he finally told me to pull off, we stopped at an adobe house on the main drag of some dusty, shit-splat town in southern California. He told me I was in for a treat: *real* Mexican food. So we went in, and saw the menu was painted on a whitewashed wall in big red letters. Words I kind of recognized, like *asada* and *cabra* next to words I didn't, like *lengüeta* and *cordero*. I was leaning towards some kind of pie (*conservó en vinagre* pies), but Tom suggested I just go with a *burrito con cabra asada*, and back on the road we went.

He wrapped himself up in his bunk and watched a couple of movies while I pressed on toward Sacramento. I munched on the massive—and delicious—burrito as I drove, half watching the road, half glancing at the reflection of the movie in my side window.

Until something began to murmur down below.

I don't know if it was a foreign spice, the quality of meat, or simply the stress and strain of the road, but my system was suddenly upset about something. I tried to get Tom's attention, but he was snoring loudly in the back and couldn't hear me. We were on a stretch of road with no lights, no shoulder, and no hope of a rest stop.

The murmur intensified over the course of 50 miles, becoming more urgent with each mile marker. And, suddenly, we came to the Interstate. We were on I-5, northbound, and the first thing I saw was a sign for a rest stop: 30 miles. I had already lasted one hour, and I was damned if I wasn't going to make it 30 minutes more. I set my teeth and kept taking deep breaths. It seemed that all of that training I had done on mid watches in the Air Force, competing with the other guys to see who could stay on the rack without going to the bathroom for the longest time, were about to pay off.

Tom woke about three miles from our destination, and I told him we were taking a little break. "That's cool, I was going to switch with you sometime, anyway. This'll work."

The rest stop was packed. Trucks lined the exit ramp, and there were no open spaces anywhere. I cruised through, barely able to control the lower half of my body, riding the clutch in anticipation.

Then I saw a spot: just to the right of a car-carrier that had gone in crooked and left himself hanging out an extra six feet. I carefully maneuvered so that I would not scrape Tom's truck on that hanging corner, and was about to breathe a deep sigh of anticipated relief... when our trailer caught on the guy to the left of us.

Tom and I leapt from the cab to see how bad it was. The other driver was out there, too; fortunately, he wasn't causing a big fuss, yet. Tom left me there, apologizing, while he straightened out and parked. Then I couldn't wait any more, and I sprinted to the bank of toilets.

The driver of the other truck determined that we hadn't done any real damage to him. I bent one of the door hinges on the trailer, but had really done more damage to my own trailer, and no one really cares much about trailers outside of the dispatch office. So Tom and I eased back onto the road, my *forgivable* mistake hanging between us. I was embarrassed, but also frightened. How could I possibly handle this job if I couldn't even get to a bathroom without causing an accident?

Tom didn't say anything for a while. He just let me stew for a few miles, and then said, "You know, you could have just stopped, put on your hazards, and hung your ass out the door anywhere along the last hundred miles." I must have looked shocked, because he laughed.

"Why not? The Swift drivers do that all the time."

2

On the Road, Again: Driving Man Part 2

Christmas came, and Tom dropped me off in Phoenix so I could go home for a holiday break. Kate picked me up and took me back to the house, while Tom pressed on back to northern California. My two weeks straddled the holiday quite nicely, a week on either side of Christmas day.

Truth be told, I spent most of that time battling some kind of horrible stomach ailment. (I had recovered from the Great Burrito Incident; this was something else.) This was my one vacation with my wife and kids at home, and I was spending that being violently ill. Neither Kate nor I said so, but between me being away and now being sick, we were starting to sour on this career choice. But we couldn't afford to let me quit. The Plan was to tough it out, soldier on, and give it one year. We would stick to the plan.

And just as I was feeling strong enough to get up, and maybe see the kids... back out on the road I went.

Tom was excited about his Christmas present: some newfangled thing called a satellite radio. Up to that point we had gotten by with his plain old AM/FM tuner (some of you kids might be old enough to remember those). That guy had programmed in every classic rock station west of Denver, and it never failed; each morning, someone was carrying *The Bob & Tom Show*. Whether it was The Thunder or The Eagle—or one odd swath of countryside presided over by The Beaver—I must have heard "Barracuda" and at least one Pink Floyd and Led Zeppelin song in each state I passed through. (If I never hear "Dream On" again, it'll be way too soon.)

"Next time we stop, I'll have to figure out how to hook this up!" he would crow, and then he'd dive under the dash and tinker while I took us on up the road. I kept offering to help. After all, I always had a knack for wiring up sound equipment. But he insisted on keeping me driving. "You need the practice!"

And practice I did. I hauled 45,000 pounds of paper down from Albany, Oregon, to the LA Times plant in Olympia, California. I found my way through Oakland, where the streets were so narrow that the buildings almost touched at the roof tops. We must have crossed Mt. Shasta at least three times, each time with a different kind of weather system: once with rain, once with snow, and once with fog so heavy, you couldn't see the drop-off on the other side of the guard rail.

I learned when to use the jake-brake, truck stop etiquette (saying "no thank you" to the local prostitutes, known as lot lizards), how to plan my fuel stops so I could get the free showers—always a top concern— and how to best pass the time when I arrived at the dock and found myself in an hours-long line to load or unload.

It was hard work, separated by enormous stretches of potentially deadly boredom. The intimidating thoughts of failure or catastrophe began to ebb, though every goof-up I made would bring them roaring back. At one point, passing through Los Angeles, I managed to wipe out one of the back tires of our trailer without noticing it.

But that had been another *forgivable* mistake; we just swapped out trailers at the lot in Fontana. Things were getting better, on the whole. I hadn't screwed up any paperwork since that first load, and had kept up on my federally regulated time logs faithfully. I was almost starting to feel good about things. And I wanted to tell someone.

I had to wait a while before we came to rest long enough to worry about calling home, and it happened that we hit a good stopping point just before New Year's. I got a shower, and a phone card, and went to call my sweetheart. I couldn't wait to hear her voice, and let her pass the phone around to the kids. So I dialed, and...

I could tell right away Kate was crying; I asked if everyone was alright. She said yeah, but something was wrong. I tried our usual in-joke. The one I used throughout her long pregnancy with Lars. He was something of a surprise, and at least once a day I found a reason to look shocked and cry out, "You mean you're pregnant??" It was especially funny in public, when she was in the third trimester and looked like she was ready to deliver right there. Guaranteed laughs!

But this time she just burst into tears. "How did you know?" she wailed.

*

I came to the table just as Tom finished ordering. The waitress was one of those fading beauties you see in places like truck stops; Tom dutifully flirted with her, and said to me as she flounced away, "Hey, did you check her out?"

"I don't dare look... I'll probably get her pregnant," I muttered. I told him about our news, but didn't tell him all of it. I left out the horrible weeks Kate had been enduring since I'd been gone again. I expected a seasoned driver would not sympathize that she was lonely while I was away, or that the kids had caught whatever I had during Christmas break before Kate herself got sick. He wouldn't want to hear about how she had not being able to contact anyone in my family for help, or that the bills were looming, or that I was terrified of what would happen if I couldn't graduate and start driving on my own. I only told him about the baby, and he made a show of counting the weeks we had been on the road to be sure it was mine. That part, Tom thought was great.

"You'll have four now?" he said, over and over. "Good thing you won't have to be around for the tough parts!" Good thing? I didn't think so.

After that, the futility of what I was doing seemed to become clear to me. My driving was alright, but I still couldn't do certain vital things by myself. The only time I successfully parked was a delivery in Twin Falls, Idaho, where we only had to pull up level with the side of the building. From there we got word that we were "deadheading" (driving an empty trailer) back down to Phoenix.

We cut down through Nevada on state highway 95. I ate the best pizza I've ever tasted in Elko. Whorehouses line the 95, it seemed, female voices on the CB offering "free showers, conversation, and *no* obligation." One place was celebrating a 25-year anniversary with discounts for club members. Another offered a frequent visitor card with some oddly worded perks.

"They're calling you, Tad!" Tom would hoot from the back of the truck. He imagined the little fingers of vapor, like in a Bugs Bunny cartoon, reaching out of the radio and leading drivers by the nose into these places.

But we drove on, not interested in the dubious goods being advertised. We pressed through the neon overload of Las Vegas; through the deep, desert dark of Parker, Arizona, and down highway 69 through Wickenburg until we passed the turnoff to my childhood home.

*

We arrived back at the terminal, and Tom shook my hand. "Hope to see you out on the road," he said. "It was a pleasure driving with you. I hope the next guy does as good a cleaning job on my truck!" We laughed, and he wandered off to do whatever it was he did.

I went on to the last stage of my apprenticeship: the big test. One of the dispatchers climbed up into a cab with me and had me drive around to put me through the paces. We hooked up to a trailer, went around the block, came back and maneuvered around the lot. Backed up, turned around... all the usual everyday things a driver needs to do.

And I failed.

"Don't worry," he said. "We can keep you on at student pay for a few more weeks and let you practice. You'll get it." Three hundred dollars a week. For a few more weeks? I thought about what I was doing. Thought about the risks... of damage... of death... and even under the best of circumstances, of simply being gone while a baby came and my kids slowly got used to me being gone. And Kate, who had been working as a security guard while I went through school, was making more money than I was making as a driver candidate.

"No thanks," I said. And, even though I had spent the better part of the last year learning to drive... I walked away.

3
Who Saved Whom

2002 was not a very good time to be us.

We moved 2,300 miles from Phoenix to Baltimore for a job, only to be told that the processing to reinstate my security paperwork would take 18 months. Sorry, they said.

I made a conscious effort to say nothing that could jeopardize a now-illusory job a year and a half in the future, and tried to figure out how to support a family of six living hand to mouth in an overpriced two-bedroom apartment.

I looked around; after all, Paul Harvey had said that in America, if you are willing to work, all you have to do is open up the want ads, and there is work available! Mr. Harvey, have you checked your want ads lately? There were jobs in there, and I was willing to work; but those jobs fell into three unsavory categories:

Jobs that required a pre-qualification I didn't have (like a specific degree or expensive certification).

"Jobs" that required an upfront investment of anywhere from $500 to $X thousand dollars. We had $30.

Jobs that didn't pay enough to buy the gas it would cost to get to them (restaurant jobs offered $3/hour; security guard $7—but they weren't hiring).

The first category was right out the window. I already owed several thousand dollars for my failed attempt at truck driving. I started putting in applications for jobs in the third category, figuring if I got several jobs it would make up for the meager wages. I even tried carpet cleaning—a category 2 and 3 job—for 13 days; but my brakes went out after putting more than 1,000 miles on the car, and I managed to make a grand total of -$130 for my troubles. I only came out ahead eventually because I could legitimately put the $800 in brake repairs on our taxes as a business expense.

In case you don't read subtext well: we were desperate. That's when the owner of a Ramada hotel took pity on me and offered me two jobs: shuttle driver and desk clerk. The pay wasn't great, but the hotel was near our apartment, and he offered me all the hours I could legally work. (Yes, there were limits—you don't want your shuttle driver dozing off.) I am still grateful to him. After a few weeks behind the desk, he decided to let me train on the night audit: a great position of trust that included a significant raise. That was where I met Wallace.

Wallace was a very neat and proper man. He was the kind of person the word "fastidious" was created for. When he tallied the receipts at the end of the night, he was fast and accurate, and scrupulously honest. The other clerks had made some remarks about him, mildly mocking but not very specific about their criticism, and he seemed somewhat scornful of them. I learned why when, after finishing his duties for the night, he pulled out his Bible and some study materials, and began to read and pray. That seemed to explain most of the attitude I had picked up on. I was familiar with the usual dynamics of a deeply religious person working amongst those who don't share his faith. I had been there myself once.

"Will this bother you?" he asked me, holding his Bible that first night. I told him it wouldn't. I had been raised in a Southern Baptist church, but had "gotten over it," I said, a little too flippantly. I felt badly, then; I try not to insult people. But I also try to discourage them from trying to save me. "I've learned a bit about 'live and let live' since my zealous youth," I told him, hoping to make both an apology and a barrier to further delving. He didn't press the issue, but after a few nights, we fell into a discussion about it.

I recognized all of the classic signs that I was being "witnessed to"; it's not a subtle thing. He led me through the usual set up, asking what I thought about Jesus and the Bible, working his way toward presenting The Choice. The way it is supposed to work is that the one being witnessed to is supposed to be backed into a corner, whether by their own ignorance of scripture, or by the patiently logical way the witness frames his questions. The Choice is that loaded question, "Why do you reject Jesus?" What it really means, though, is, "Why do you reject me and my belief system?"

I let him lead me through to the point where he asked me, "Do you know what will happen to your soul when you die?"

"Not to be rude," I said, "but isn't that between me and God?"

"Well, yes," he said. "I am just concerned that you might not know what you're missing in your life."

"I know all too well what I'm missing; but there isn't a church out there that is going to support my family for me. Letting a particular group of people into my head to tell me what I should and shouldn't do, or think, isn't going to get me a better job or a cheaper apartment. I am quite satisfied with the state of my relationship with the Creator of the Universe, and I don't see a need to give other people a way to manipulate my mind."

He blinked.

"Look," I continued, "I have nothing against you, and if what you are studying and learning is helpful to you, and makes it easier for you to make good choices and cope with your life, then please, continue doing it. But in my experience, even the most well-intentioned religion aims to control the individual members through their doctrine and through their social structure. It amounts to brainwashing, and no matter how benign or well-intentioned it may be, I have no use for it. I have spent years trying to free myself of outside claims on my soul, and I'm not about to give that up now."

He blinked again. Then he said, "I understand completely. But the last thing we would want to do is 'brainwash' you!"

This was a lie.

He smiled, and pushed a packet of photocopied pages from his study book toward me. "Here; take these. They are little prayers that I read, and what I suggest you do is take them home, and read them over and over again. And while you're reading, try to believe what you are reading as hard as you can. You'll see, after about 25 times, the truth of the words will start to sink in!"

He looked proud, as though he had brilliantly countered all of my years of struggle with myself and with my family, and had answered the innermost questions of my soul. He didn't look like a pusher of poisonous ideas. He didn't look at all like a man who had just proven my deepest qualms about religion, and justified my discomfort with evangelism.

I looked at the packet he had given me. "I am a sinner, without value." That was the first line. "Nothing I do can save me." It went on; it got worse. There was even a version of the old "Footprints" poem—the one where the writer accuses God of not walking beside him as he walks along the beach (the symbol of his life), and God tells him, "That is when I was carrying you."

Most of these were words I had grown up with; words I had worked hard to believe, hating myself for hating their trite smugness. They were words that had caused me unbelievable pain, because I was afraid to disappoint the people who had taught them to me.

I looked back at Wallace, and I could feel the anger welling up. I wanted to throw the papers back at him, and scream my frustration in his face. I wanted to make him understand that if I went down that path again—if I started believing I had no value again—it would destroy me. But he was there, telling me about his life, and how this church of his had broken through his ego and helped him overcome his self-destructive past. It was the same old testimony I had heard from hundreds of people while growing up, and I hated that he was trying to use it on me again.

But, I saw that he needed that crutch. He needed that faith in something outside himself. He needed to believe that his morality was enforced by something greater than himself, or he wouldn't be able to stick with it. If I let him, he would try to convince me that I didn't deserve credit for keeping my own life together, and while I wasn't about to let him do that to me... who was I to kick his crutch out from under him?

"I'll take these home, and let you know how it goes," I said. He patted my hand. The gesture reminded me of my grandfather, who used to pull us kids aside and whisper small sermons in our ears until he was satisfied he had taught us something. We all got good at smiling and nodding, mouthing whatever platitudes would show Grandpa how devout we were, so we could go back to playing. I did that to Wallace, now, too.

A few weeks later, I managed to find a position with a defense contractor that doubled what I was making at the hotel. With the overtime available, we would be able to pay all of our bills, *and* start to dig out of the crater that the transition from Air Force life had left in our bank book. The owner of the hotel was a very kind about the fact that he was losing an employee he had taken a risk on and invested in, and I tried to express how much I appreciated what he had done for me. On my way out the door of the hotel, Wallace shook my hand, and beamed. He said something about God providing, if we just believe in Him. I smiled, and nodded, and walked out the door.

I left Wallace there with his God, and I walked on alone. If there were any footprints left next to mine, I couldn't see them in the concrete.

But I didn't waste any more time looking for them. I had work to do.

4
But, Before I Go...

Working with Wallace was only half of my job at the hotel. In order to pay for both food *and* rent, I needed all the hours I could get, so the owner let me work extra shifts driving the airport shuttle. I still had my CDL from Arizona, so the insurance and other paperwork were a snap.

The Baltimore-Washington International Airport was not as nearby as people were led to believe by the hotel's advertising literature. Instead of being located a block away across the train tracks, on the road lined with hotels of all brands, chains, and price levels, our hotel was nearly six miles away. Technically it was located at the far west edge of the "BWI Hotel District," so that was how it was advertised.

My passengers unanimously found that literature quite deceptive, and they made sure to tell me so as the van rolled out of the terminal and away from the bright lights of the clearly visible hotel strip to pull onto the wooded Baltimore-Washington Parkway. Depending on my mood or the language abilities of the passengers, I would either benignly ignore them, sympathetically commiserate with them, or distract them. I preferred to do the latter.

"What those other hotels don't tell you is that there are some rather dangerous animals at loose on hotel strip," I told one group. "The government has a secret lab one block over where they do genetic manipulation, and sometimes the things they make get loose and run straight for the neon. One time they were working on a super-soldier program, and they accidentally set loose a *sasquatch*. It ate some lady's poodle and busted into the Hampton Inns. When the military police found it, it was sleeping curled up in the hotel's jacuzzi. They're still pulling hair out of the filter of that thing."

I didn't pull out the sasquatch story unless I was sure I could get away with it. Having military people in the van helped, and if I knew my passengers were from Canada or Australia, they usually got a kick out of that one. The elderly or business travelers did not. Small children and teenagers did not; kids in that magical in-between space usually did.

That part of the job was the first thing about being back in America that felt good, right, and normal again. Things were still tight financially and there were a lot of uncomfortable questions about our immediate future, but having this job allowed me to begin to put my failure at trucking, the stress of moving, and the uncertainty about our latest pregnancy into perspective. Having a job I could do and feel confident doing made me feel like the bad things could be dealt with, and we could prepare for this little good thing that was fast approaching.

All summer, while I worked, Kate fretted over the children. We still needed the government WIC vouchers, and the state children's health care program just to cover the basics of feeding and immunizing them for school; and she was rather desperate to get our precocious Séamus into the Head Start program because he had shown so much eagerness to begin reading.

As Kate's belly grew, Bria, who was five, became intensely interested in the concept of babies, and kept asking for a baby sister for her birthday. Kate tried to explain that we didn't know whether we would have a baby brother or sister—though we were all hoping for another girl to balance out the group—and we had no idea when the baby would come, but she assured our eldest that she would do the best she could.

Since I was spending so much time at the hotel, or in the van, I took the cell phone to work with me. Considering my history with telephones, I did not like the cell phone either, and when I wore it clipped to my belt, I had a tendency to catch it on things. Usually, it would pop off of my hip and skitter out into the road while I was loading or unloading passengers.

I took to leaving the phone plugged into the cigarette lighter, and propped it prominently in the cup holder. As the pending due date approached, I began pointing it out to my passengers as I rolled out onto the parkway.

"I don't mean to be rude, but if this phone rings during our trip today, you will all be joining me at the Anne Arundel Medical Center in beautiful Annapolis!" I was kidding, of course, but that was a great conversation starter. It was almost as useful a story as the sasquatch.

One unexpected consequence of saying this to people was a spike in my tips. Most of the time, this was a subtle thing. I would point to the phone and deliver my ice-breaker line; the passengers would ask the usual questions, and when I dropped them and their bags off at our destination, they would press an extra few dollars into my hand. I mentioned this to Kate, and she got embarrassed.

"I feel like we're exploiting our baby!" she protested.

"No, it's not like that at all!" I said. "I'm not telling people this so they'll give me money. It's just that I'm excited! Of course, I'll be driving tomorrow afternoon, if you want to call at some point... I'll bet that would set a record one-day total!"

Not everyone was impressed with my pending baby or my mythical Army mutant stories. In any job dealing with the public, there are always haters. I think my worst one was the lady who asked the front desk for a ride to the mall. It was a slow day, and it was during the early-afternoon lull between the last of the late check-outs and the earliest of the arriving flights.

I helped her into the van, and she climbed all the way into the back seat. It was just the two of us, so I had offered the front seat, but she insisted. Then she proceeded to shout questions at me about the mall that I couldn't answer.

"Do they have a good shoe outlet? What movies are they showing? How many jewelry stores are there?"

Kate and I took the kids to that mall all the time, since it didn't cost anything to walk around and people watch, but I couldn't answer this lady's questions. I told her I didn't do a lot of jewelry shopping. She made a face at the movie titles I could remember. I said I thought maybe the Bass Pro Shop sold shoes.

She had me drop her off near the Medieval Times, and I expected not to see her for a while; but when I pulled back into the hotel parking lot and entered the lobby, I was told to turn right back around and go pick her up in front of the theater.

The woman was positively steaming when she climbed back into the van.

"Was anything wrong?" I asked.

"Yes!" she exclaimed. "I didn't expect to be left in a den of Satan!"

"Really? When did that open?"

"Have you ever *been* to that movie theater?"

"Yes, ma'am...?"

"Have you not noticed the idols to Satan? They're all over the lobby!" She pointed out the window at the theater's massive Egyptian-themed facade. "And those *statues*!"

"Ma'am, that's supposed to be a pyramid. Those are just Egyptian gods."

"False gods!" she crowed. "The devil!"

She railed against idols and the horrible offenses she had suffered at the hands of our awful mall the whole way back to the hotel. The trip was only half a mile, but it felt longer.

That lady was a rarity, though. Most folks were just tired and happy to be on the ground; they were content to snooze or chat with me, or laugh at my dumb jokes.

At home, though, Kate was getting tense and eager to have this baby. She was feeling healthier with this baby than she had with the last pregnancy. Lars, whom she had nicknamed "Firecracker" in the womb, had been very large and very late. Not only had we had to contend with a false alarm and an extra trip, driving across English farmland, but Kate had come down with some kind of virus, so she was running a fever of 102 when he was finally born.

This new baby had earned the nickname "Live Wire," but other than being active, this one had not brought on the same degree of fatigue and weight gain as the last one had. The pregnancy wasn't nearly as difficult as the rest of our life in a small, two-bedroom apartment and with three small, energetic kids. My long hours, low pay, and the uncertainty of being able to keep making ends meet combined with Kate's sense of isolation in the apartment to strain her nerves.

The low point came the night I got home after a long shift of driving and training for the night desk. Normally, when I came in the door, there was light and noise and food. Kate loves to bake, and hates to let kids vegetate in front of the TV when they could be doing something fun, so most evenings they spent making dinner and either some kind of dessert or crafts together.

On this night, though, most of the lights were off, the TV was on, and Bria and Séamus were sitting quietly and watching it.

"Where's Mommy?" I asked. They pointed to the back bedroom, where Kate and I had set up our room and a bassinet for the new baby.

"What's she doing?" I asked.

"Crying," Bria said, matter of factly.

As it happened, after sending Bria and Séamus off to school, and running errands all morning, Kate had put baby Lars down for a nap, and fallen asleep herself for a bit. He was almost eighteen months old, so when he woke up before she did and noticed that his diaper was full, he decided to lever himself out of his crib and travel the house, spreading the news of what was in his diaper as he went.

He wasn't walking, yet, and he wasn't a crawler. Lars liked to roll. So as his mom snored in the back room, he rolled out of his room, through the kitchen, and under the dining room table. Along the way, he smeared a brown Van Gogh painting on the carpet and walls to mark his path, dragging whatever toys or stuffed animals he encountered with him. By the time she woke up, he had fallen asleep again under the table in a pile of shit-smeared toys.

He had not made a sound.

I learned later, when Kate could bring herself to speak of this, that she had stepped out of our room to go start dinner, and found the disgusting tableau. She described the scene without emotion, and said only that she "cleaned him up and put him to bed," but the absence of feces when I arrived clearly meant that she had done a lot of cleaning before retreating to our room. Understandably, I became responsible for dinner that night, and Lars sat quietly in his crib, wisely not complaining at the disrupted routine.

A dozen years later, we do not tell this story when Kate is in the room, because her eyes go dim and she looks off into the far distance as a single tear rolls down her cheek.

At long last, the day came. I got a phone call while I was pulling into the parking lot with a group of passengers, and gave an excited whoop. It was the end of my shift, anyway, and they gave me a record-breaking tip. I couldn't tell whether that meant "Congratulations" or "Thank you for dropping us off, first!"

Kate and I left our kids in the capable hands of our neighbors and made our way to the hospital. Of the four children, this was hands down the easiest birth. The hospital was clean and relaxed, and the baby was our littlest.

Kate had processed an application at her security firm from someone named whose first name was Mileidy, and that name quickly topped our list of choices. We named the new baby Mileidy, partly because we thought the name was beautiful, and partly because we figured it was inevitable. She was the dainty princess of the group from day one, deserving of the title: *m'lady*, indeed. A new baby was sure to be the demanding youngest, waited upon hand and tiny foot.

She was healthy, and Kate was healthy, and while we knew there would be a lot of work ahead of us to get from where we were to where we needed to be, we were just glad to have our whole family together.

Mileidy was born at 8 p.m., and the next morning we took her home in time to present her to Bria, who got the baby sister she wanted that morning for her sixth birthday.

5

Eleven Thoughts at 11:11 on 11/11

Well, I thought about the Army,
Dad said, "Son, you're fucking high!"
So I thought, yeah, there's a first for everything,
And I took my old man's advice.
                    -    Ben Folds Five, "Army"

1) My son, Séamus, was born at 11:11 p.m. For weeks after his birth, every time I saw a clock it was 11:11, so I got in the habit of whispering to myself, "Happy Birthday, son," whenever I saw that time displayed. After a while, I started to feel like it was eleven after eleven every time I looked at a clock. I whispered a "Happy Birthday" to him almost every day for his first five years.

2) I mentioned this to Brent, who lived in Texas. He's a veteran of the Army, and a former Russian linguist like myself. He's not what you would think of when you say "veteran"; he's a skinny kid with long, black hair; a guitar player, a coffee drinker, a philosopher. He got out after four years, realizing that the Army wasn't interested in what he had to offer. The feeling was mutual. He told me the number 11 is pretty important in numerology, and that the lead singer of a band called Fate's Warning was captivated enough with it to compose a song called "The Eleventh Hour," dealing with the idea of portents and memory, and weaving in musical symbols based on the number.

3) On November 11, one is not supposed to be thinking about little boys' birthdays and heavy metal bands; one is supposed to be

thinking about veterans. In America, though, Veterans Day is relatively watered down. We try to cram the remembrance of all of our veterans into just one day. The UK and the rest of Europe still call it "Remembrance Day," and it is heavily associated with World War I. They remember to wear poppies in their lapels (not to mention remembering *why* they wear poppies in their lapels) and they have a moment of silence at the moment the Armistice ending the War went into effect: "the eleventh hour of the eleventh day of the eleventh month" of 1918. Of course, if they tried to remember their veterans from every war *they've* ever fought, it would require more than one day; perhaps as many as eleven.

4) In the spirit of the US holiday, though, I try to think about as many of them as possible. Remembering veterans has become a lot easier for me over the years. Doing the family tree has given me a lot to remember. My dad was a medical specialist in the National Guard; my uncle was in Vietnam. Both of my grandfathers were in World War II; a great-grandfather was in WWI, his father was in an Ohio Regiment in the Civil War along with his brothers and cousins. I've found ancestors that were in service in wars that Americans (Spanish-American and Mexican Wars) and Britons (War of 1812) have all but forgotten about entirely. When I dwell on the breadth of service others have given, it is still a shock to me to be reminded that I am a veteran, too.

5) I don't feel like a veteran. I never experienced any kind of combat. My time in service was often more like *Stripes* than *Sands of Iwo Jima* or *Pearl Harbor*. I'm not complaining, but I relate more to Dilbert than to John Wayne. Lieutenant Dan swinging from the rigging of Forrest Gump's shrimp boat seems more veteran-like than I do. Maybe it's his missing limbs; I'm just an overweight schlub with authority issues and an over-developed grasp of acronyms.

6) Kate, also a veteran, tells me that I should be proud that I served at all, since so few step up voluntarily. I am proud; I'm just humble about it. It feels weird to honor myself, and I certainly don't expect anyone else to do it. I don't feel like what I did was terribly

special, compared to all of the more competent people around me. I try to prove my worth as an observer, remembering the people I served with, who had done so many worthwhile things with their military careers. My wife and I try to talk about them on these occasions, and give the kids a sense of the respect we have for those in the military, then and now.

7) Part of my unease with my veteran status probably comes from knowing that despite the lip service paid to our military, and the fetishized fervor with which Americans treat the flag and the Pledge of Allegiance and other such symbols, they don't treat actual veterans nearly as well. They're too willing to ignore them when they come back broken, and they're far too eager to send them away to be broken in the first place. The only reason we have benefits at all is because the veterans of World War I formed the "Bonus Army" and camped out on the Capital Mall in Washington DC in 1932, at the height of the Great Depression. They got called "communists" and were accused of being unpatriotic. And President Hoover sent General Douglas Macarthur to evict them from DC. That makes it easier to ignore chicken hawk trolls on Twitter.

8) I didn't know about that history when I left the Air Force, but even if I had, I still would have opted not to apply for Veteran's Administration benefits. I knew people who claimed benefits, and collected surprisingly ample checks for injuries that had nothing to do with combat. I fell down while playing volleyball for PT, and my shoulder still gives me trouble sometimes, but not having to fight for incremental financial support is far more valuable to me. I prefer to think that the drunk who fell out of bed after a hard night of partying and broke a tailbone is the exception. I'd rather think that a real Wounded Warrior is getting a little bit more with less effort because I'm not cluttering the system with my silly claim.

9) It's important to keep the focus of any discussion about veterans squarely on the people who turn up for emergencies. My brother-in-law's unit was based at McGuire AFB in New Jersey; just a bunch of mechanics, but they were called up to New York City on the

morning of September 11, 2001, and he was a couple of blocks outside of the danger zone when the second tower fell. Six months earlier, and I could still have been called up. As soon as you take the oath, you're obligated to go where you're needed. Come what may.

10) We all know how uncertain the future is. That's why our species takes so much comfort from remembering the past. Whatever happened before, however horrific, is at least known. We look for patterns and try to predict what will happen next. Symbols are comforting; numbers are symbols, like 11:11 and all of its associated implications. Maybe it really means something that Séamus was born at that time. Maybe it's some kind of sign that he'll grow up and follow in the long, unspoken family tradition of service. Of course, he could decide to wear a pink tutu on his head, call himself "Mr. Booty," and sing songs about his own butt for a living. That's what he did yesterday, and you know how insidious some patterns can be. We'll just have to love him no matter what.

11) These thoughts, and others less focused, churned through my mind all day on November 11. As I crawled into bed that night, I kissed the veteran lying next to me—already asleep, so my snoring wouldn't disturb her—and I checked to make sure my alarm was set. Of course, the time was 11:11.

I settled onto my side and whispered, "Happy Birthday, son."
And happy Veterans Day.

6
Decant the Midnight Lizard

I plunge my face into my pillow and feel the cool fabric leach the heat from my strained and weary eyes. Clouds of the sandman's magic dust puff up around me, and I am already sailing away into a dream and relaxing into my pose of repose, which is not unlike that of the Coyote upon reaching the canyon floor in a Roadrunner cartoon.

"Did you empty the boy?" The voice of my lovely bride jerks to a halt my descent into slumber, and my body goes rigid as I fight my way back into wakefulness. I should have known I was forgetting something.

Lars is three, and took to toilet training like a donut to coffee. The only problem he has is remembering to get up in the night to avoid drowning. It has become my job to empty him once before going to bed, and again in the morning before I leave for work. I don't mind, except that he is an extremely heavy sleeper, as the twinge in my back will attest. I've lobbied against the nightly *dink o'walla* with all my heart, but have been consistently out-voted. I seem to be the only one who has made a connection between the 2.5 ounces of water he drinks just before bed and the 2.5 gallon deluge that issues forth from him between 10 p.m. and 4 a.m.

So, it falls to me as the last one down and the first one up to enforce the head call. If I don't do it, he will awaken, cold and sticky, forty minutes before my alarm is set to go off, and will climb into our bed with his soggy drawers. The changing of sheets and pajamas (his and ours, now), and the wailing and crying (his and ours), and the rinsing off of his soiled body and tucking him into his remade bed generally leaves me with ten minutes until I have to get up again. Not enough time to get any more rest, and too much time to sit and dawdle over my cereal.

This night, I am especially tired. The cold I have been fighting has resorted to guerilla tactics for the last couple of weeks: gone during the workweek, but suddenly appearing on Friday night. Sometimes it's in my sinuses, sometimes in my throat, sometimes in my eye. I think it has a secret base in my liver, so I've been using the Russian remedy: one shot of vodka with a dash of pepper.

I drag myself down the hall and grope about in his bed, looking for him. He is a small boy, and the bed seems large in the dark; he could be anywhere! He isn't. I am about to give in and turn on a light when I feel something underfoot. It *is* a foot. It is attached to the wee lad, who has made a nest under his bed out of stuffed animals, dump trucks, and a few Justice League action figures. Batman, devotedly standing guard, dives cowl-first onto my foot as I lift the boy like a sack of rice, and with a stifled yelp, I begin hopping painfully toward the bathroom, all while trying to keep a good grip on him.

Not many people fully appreciate how floppy the body of a sleeping child can be until they try to pick one up in the middle of the night. This one sags in the middle as I prop his head on my shoulder and drape his legs over the elbow of the other arm. It isn't a problem until he startles awake and begins to writhe like a cat in a bathtub. I manage to prevent him from slamming his head into the door frame by slamming my head into the door frame. He will have an interesting vocabulary by the time he begins school. The blast of cranial pain distracts from the Bat-marks in my foot, though, and that helps me maintain my balance.

"Sh-sh-shh!" I say, trying to sooth him back into immobility. He relaxes a little bit, then suddenly drops back to sleep. I complete the journey to the bathroom with only minor limping, and try to stand him up on the little stool next to the toilet. His legs won't go down. They waver bonelessly. They curl up under him, and he tucks his chin to his chest and throws his arms up, giving me nothing to hold onto. He almost slips away, but I manage to grab him by the elbows and haul him back up.

Now he's mad, and his legs shoot out as he explodes with furious activity. He is a whirlwind, a wolverine cornered, a many-tentacled rage beast desperate to get away from me.

Then, with a plop, all action stops. Something awful has happened. We stand there in the darkness, until realization dawns. He tears the night apart with his shrill, angry scream: "It's CO-O-O-OLD!!"

He has planted his left foot squarely into the toilet bowl.

Yanking his foot free, he begins kicking savagely, liberally spraying toilet water hither and yon. Fortunately, it didn't get on his clothing, since it was busy soaking into all of mine. After a brief tussle, I wrestle him up onto the sink, and jam his foot under the tap. I wash him, pat him dry, and stand him up—finally—on his stool. There, he proceeds to pee for an eternity.

I have time to wash myself up, dry, mop up the floor, check the pipes for wear, tidy the tub toys, and re-grout the tile. When he is done, I gently carry him back to his room, and place him softly in his bed, where he is supposed to be. I kiss him gently on the forehead and whisper, "Sweet dreams."

When he whispers it back to me, all is forgiven, and I limp gratefully back to my own, sweet, welcoming bed.

7

"I Love You Anyway"

My younger son's name is Lars, but I sometimes called him "Thor" because he often used his head as a hammer. He was determined to put up a fight, no matter what. He's getting better, now that he has passed out of that 3-to-5-year-old phase that all boys seem to go through—you know, the one where God sends Gabriel to ask you to keep it down—but he still likes to show his gums every now and then and really resist something. He used to do it with meals, refusing to eat for hours then howling about how hungry he was at bedtime. Until recently, he was very consistent about revolting at cleaning-up time, to the point that we took away *all* of the toys for a week.

But through it all, we gritted our teeth and did our duty as parents. We argued, fought, and regretfully followed through on even the most dire of threats (such as the Week Without Toys), making sure to stress the point throughout: you will do your part in this house. Heck, even I eventually learned that lesson, with Kate's patient help.

And at night, when we were all exhausted and ready to chuck each other out the windows, we would tuck him in, sweating from conflict and hoarse from shouting down toddler arguments, and tell him, "I love you."

Most people don't think about this, but "love" is one of those English words that works as more than one part of speech. It is a noun, of course, as in, "You are my love," or, "Our love burns hotter than fire." It is also a verb, as in, "I will love you forever," or, "I don't love you anymore" (two phrases that are often spoken by the same mouth to the same audience, with a noticeable lack of "forever" in between).

Loving your child is not optional, though; it's like driving without insurance. You must love the child or there are terrible consequences in your future. But like the insurance analogy, you have to choose it. Whether you go with Gecko Love, or State Farm, it is always a conscious decision to love, in the end.

Love, after all, is an Action Verb.

While tucking him in, we told Lars, "I love you," and he would usually say, with all of the hatred a young child could muster, "Well I don't love you!" We talked about ways to handle that: ignoring it at first, and then growing more concerned when he kept it up. We didn't want to make yet another battle out of it, and we certainly didn't want to force him to say "I love you" back to us, especially if he was angry about it. Rounds of therapy lie down *that* path, young Padawan.

So we took to giving him the answer, "I love you, anyway."

This drove him up the wall. He hated that answer. The first few times we tried this strategy, he flew into a screaming rage, bellowing, "Well, I *don't* love *you*!!!" He was chastised for yelling, and tucked back into bed, and told (as calmly as possible), "It doesn't matter if you love me or not; I love you, anyway."

Perhaps you've heard of those people who respond to angry drivers and their fingers with a cheerful, "Have a nice day!" or, "God bless you, too!" Those people describe the feeling they get from that moment as being both rebellious and provocative (because it throws off the angry person at the other end) and very fulfilling (because you aren't the one committing an angry or hateful act). That was how it felt to us; like we were waving and smiling at a fuming jerk in a souped-up Civic, speeding on his way to a date with a radar gun up the road.

But as satisfying as that is, and as right as we felt not to force the issue, there remained a sense that we weren't getting through to him. At the end of the day, he wasn't a rude stranger on the road; he was our son. And he was using our own affection against us. We decided that he knew it was a weapon, and he was simply going to keep using it on us until he got tired of it. The only reasonable way to get him to stop was to outlast him.

So, I got used to the routine. Kate and I tucked them each in, and gave them all hugs and kisses; and when we got to Lars and told him we loved him, he scowled and said, "I don't love you." We gave our reply, and went upstairs. Tonight, I was especially braced for it, since I was parenting alone and I'd cut short whatever game the kids were playing and did a forced march through the house to gather all of the Legos they had strewn about. (Don't start me on the dangers of Lego-mining.) With Mommy out of town, Daddy was the least popular substitute sheriff ever.

I got medicine for the sick ones, and water for all; I tucked in special blankets and buddies, adjusted the bedtime electrical devices—lights, off; fan and dehumidifier, on—and gave the round of hugs. I got to Lars' bed, and as per usual asked him to calm down and lie still. I hugged him, and told him I loved him, and he said, "I love you, too, Daddy."

"Well, I love you any...way..." I looked down at him, and he was grinning at me like a loon.

"I knew you were going to say that," he said.

I left it at that.

8
Why Skeletons Don't Have Kids...

Here is a small sample of life in our car. You won't get the full effect unless you read the parts aloud—very loud—and have a Greek chorus of gigglers accompanying you:

Dad: What a great dinner out at our neighborhood family restaurant.

Mom: Yes, and such amusing holiday-themed activity books for the kids!

Eldest daughter, age 8: Hey! It's got jokes in it! "Where do elves keep their money?"

Mom: In a snow bank.

Eldest: Ha, ha! That's right!

Big Brother, age 5: Mommy! How did you know?

Little Brother, age 3: Knock, knock!

Little Princess, age 2: (shrieks with laughter)

Mom: I'm older than you, I know things.

Eldest: "What do snowmen eat for breakfast?"

Little Bro: Knock, Knock!

Dad: Cereal flakes?

Big Bro: Who's there?

Princess: Eeeeeeeee!!

Eldest: That's right, Dad! Gee, you guys are smart!

Mom: Enjoy that while she still says it.

Dad: No kidding! I like people who are easily impressed with me.

Little Bro: KNOCK, KNOCK!!!

Big Bro: Somebody ask him "who's there"!

Mom: Who's there, honey?

Little Bro: Uh.... POOP! Ha ha ha ha ha...

Princess: Poop! Aieeeeeee!

Dad: Oy...

Big Bro: Why didn't the skeleton cross the road?

Eldest: Hey, that's not on there... They're supposed to be Christmas jokes!

Dad: Why didn't the skeleton cross the road, Schmoo?

Eldest: But that's a Halloween joke! It's Christmas!

Big Bro: Because he had no guts!

Princess: Poopy guts! Ha ha ha ha....

Little Bro: Knock, knock!

Mom: Oh, nice.

Eldest: Why did the elephant stand on the marshmallow?

Dad: Huh?

Little Bro: KNOCK KNOCK!

Dad: Oh, God...

Mom: Why did the elephant stand on the marshmallow, darlin'?

Big Bro: Who's there?

Little Bro: KNOCK KNOCK!

Dad: Who's there, already!

Princess: Knock, knock!

Eldest: So he wouldn't fall in the cocoa!

(silence)

Big Bro: Cocoa? Ohhh.... I get it! Ha ha ha!

Little Bro: Knock, knock!

Mom: *sigh* Who's there?

Little Bro: Cocoa

Mom & Dad: Cocoa who?

(silence)

Little Bro: Uh... POOPY CHOCOLATE!! (pronounced "ch-LOCK-it")

Unison: HA, HA, HA, HA, HA!

Dad: Good grief...

Mom: Oh, good... we're home...

Princess: (chanting) Poopy, poopy, chocolate, chocolate...

Mom (to Dad): Is this really our life?

Dad: I'm afraid so.

Mom: Can we complain to somebody?

Dad: No one would believe us.

Little Bro: Uh... POOPY CHOCOLATE!!

Mom & Dad: ENOUGH!!

Answer to the title: Because they have no guts.

9

Coyote Falls Again

Saturday, June 28, 2008

"Most people leave in the summer, you know," Dad said with a grin. "They don't come for vacation to escape the mild climate back home."

"But it doesn't feel that hot," I told him. And I meant it, too. It was 115 degrees Fahrenheit, but I didn't feel hot. I could feel the pressure of the heat on my arms, but that was all it was—a little pressure.

I know about the dangers of the heat. I grew up in Phoenix, after all. Kate, the kids, and I came prepared with camel packs for carrying water, extra sunscreen, light clothing, hats, and plans that called for days full of swimming, hiking, driving, and fun sandwiched between days of visiting and sipping cool drinks in the air conditioning.

"And you really want to move back here?" he asked, incredulously.

The thing is, I did; but we tried moving from Baltimore back to Phoenix five years before and failed. I'd have to make sure I did it right this time, and I wanted to be sure that I had a job lined up—preferably one I liked as much as my current job in Baltimore—and that all of the other things important to us were possible: visiting with family, touring the National parks, catching the occasional baseball game. I wanted to settle in Arizona, but I didn't want to settle *for* Arizona.

It is a big state, and we wanted to see a lot of it on this visit. Kate and I budgeted for a rental car and plenty of gasoline; we drove without the air on to conserve a bit, and to revel in the dryness and the scents of creosote and blooming cacti. Kate luxuriated in the sun, darkening her skin and lightening her hair—taking proper care to apply sunscreen, naturally.

The weather was a bit cooler up at the Grand Canyon, where we spent three days (two to travel, one to soak up the splendor) in the middle of the trip. Trading pine trees for creosote and lopping 20 degrees off the thermometer definitely helps survive the high summer.

Sunset was a priority at the Canyon. Kate had photographic ambitions and wanted to get some shots of the sun going down on that particular horizon. My job was to keep the children from running along (off) the edge while she focused on her task. I grabbed the two smaller ones, and they immediately protested.

"Wait, what do you see out there?" I asked excitedly, pointing west. "What's that?"

"It's the sun. Now let me go!" protested our little blond Hercules, aka Lars.

"But what's it made of?" I asked. Mileidy, the little princess, was sulking on my lap, but I knew if I could get Lars to answer me, I'd have his attention.

"Burning hot gas," he said.

"Right, but what does it look like it's made of?"

"Gold?" answered Séamus, settling on my other side.

"It does," I said. "In fact, that's what Coyote thought it was made of. That's why he built those wings. But you guys already know about all that."

"No, we don't!" they cried. "What wings?"

I told them how Coyote, who spent most of his days trotting around in the desert, looking for something to eat or for someone to play a trick on, tried to fly to the Sun to steal the big, gleaming pile of gold when it touched the horizon. He knew he couldn't jump high enough to get to the Sun when it was high overhead, but it occurred to him that he should be able to get to it when it set each evening. At first, I had to explain, it was very frustrating for Coyote to figure out where the Sun would touch down. He would watch it set, mark the place with landmarks, and spend all the next day trying to get to the spot where it had landed, only to have it come down somewhere else each night!

He followed the Sun for weeks and weeks, until he came to the rim of the Canyon, and here—on the very spot where we were sitting!—he gave up. "I'll never figure out where the Sun is going to set if it keeps changing every night," he said, and he sat and watched the condors flying high above him, so much closer to the Sun than he'd ever be able to get. The next night, while he tried to figure out how to trick one of the condors into landing next to him for dinner, he noticed that the sun was setting on the lip of the Canyon across from him. And it was setting in the very same spot as the night before!

Now this is where Coyote showed how clever he was; he realized that if he tried to get over to that spot during the day, the Sun would see him, and would just set somewhere else. He would need to lurk off to the side and then pounce at the last minute. But how to get across that huge Canyon and surprise the Sun?

That was when he got the idea to copy the condors. He went around the desert, gathering sticky pitch and yucca leaves all day, and stuck the leaves together to make big wings that he could fit on his arms and back. Then he waited until the sun began to settle down on the rim across from him. He ran out to the edge and leapt high, catching the strong winds that up-drafted from the river at the bottom of the Canyon.

Coyote soared high and fast across the Canyon, startling the condors and confusing a cottontail that happened to look up just then. (The cottontail was so scared that he dove into his warren and started digging down so far that he eventually went blind and became a mole.) Coyote only saw his prize ahead of him, though. He reached out, greedily ready to snatch up as much gold as he could grab... but the closer he got to the Sun, the hotter it got.

And, of course, you know what happened. The pitch melted, and his wings fell apart, and Coyote fell just short of his goal. Down, down, down into the river at the bottom of the Canyon he fell with a plop.

"Now, you would think Coyote would give up, but he still tries to get that gold. And sometimes, he thinks of a new way to make wings or some other trick to launch himself across the Canyon, so if you sit still and watch carefully, you might see him leap out there tonight."

They all looked out, just as I'd suggested; even the 11-year-old Bria, who was still recovering from the disappointment of not being invited to attend Hogwarts School of Witchcraft and Wizardry last year. We all watched as tourists snapped photos of squirrels and each other, and leaned precariously over rails and ledges. We watched the birds swirl far below us, and the tiny twist of river turned into molten copper.

"I see him!" cried Mileidy, pointing. There was nothing there, but they all started shouting and laughing until the sun was all the way down. And Kate returned from her few moments of peace snapping her photos.

A couple of days later, we were at the Phoenix Zoo, where we were pleasantly surprised to see most of the animals awake and roaming around their pens despite the already oppressive heat. There were two shy coyotes skulking around in their area, but Mileidy had trouble spotting them until one came right up to the front and stopped to watch the human exhibit for a bit. When she saw him, she got very excited, and leaned forward to stage whisper at him:

"Next time, go for the *moon*! It's silver, and won't melt you!"

She's a wise one, that littlest little.

10

The Snip: A Public Service Announcement

Warning: Severe Ick Factor Ahead!

If you are bothered by discussions of medical procedures, bodily fluids, or patient-eye views of urology, then I suggest you skip to another chapter. It's probably very rude of me to recount these events, but I consider this tale to be a public service announcement, and so I'm going to post it anyway.

I told Bernie the boss, "I'm going to be out Wednesday, and I won't be back until Monday."

My friend Paul asked why I was going to be out (me, the guy known for working 72+ hours a week)... and I told him: it was time for the vasectomy.

"Are you *nuts*?" he shouted, then his cheeks colored and he shuffled off.

I understood how he felt; he was a single guy with all of his silly macho ideals still intact. But Kate and I had four little kids in rapid succession. Due mainly to drug and latex allergies, other options for population control weren't viable. It was hard to make the leap, but we decided we'd both make sure that *it* couldn't happen again. And I was going first.

I went to the evaluation appointment, not sure what to expect. I did *not* expect a very cute, pixie-faced female doctor to explain my choices for the procedure in graphic detail while fanning illustrations of the options on penis flashcards before her face. She showed me the three basic methods:

1. Two scalpel incisions, one directly over each tube.

2. Two incisions made with sharpened shears (jab shears through skin, open shears to make a 1/4 inch opening).

3. One scalpel incision in the middle, and fish out the tubes with a probe.

She saw I had turned green, so she showed me the list of six doctors in the practice. "They will each perform whichever method you prefer—except Dr. Herzinger; he only does the sharpened shears. He says it heals better with a ragged incision." That's right, it was pronounced Dr. HURT-zinger. I could not have made that up if I tried.

In the end, guess who was the only doc available for the foreseeable future?

So I showed up the day of, having shaved as instructed. This was an awkward thing for me, and I followed the instructions precisely, marveling to myself that people would do this optionally. And regularly. Feeling more exposed than I had since puberty, I lay on the table, only to have the doctor shake his ancient head and say with sad disapproval, "Didn't do a very thorough job there, did you?" Then he seized a straight razor and deftly cleared half an acre between my legs that I had never seen before. (Strictly speaking, I still haven't seen it.)

Once I was completely shorn, and utterly humiliated, the anesthetizing began. Have you had a dental procedure done? The doctor jabs in the needle, and then slowly wiggles it around while injecting cold poison; in this procedure, that sensation was compounded by the feeling of my testicle being inflated to the size of a basketball. I white-knuckled the sides of the gurney, and just as I was certain he had decided to dispense with the planned incisions and instead just *pop* the bastard... he stopped. I released my breath and my grip, grateful it had ended without any hitting or screaming. The doc nodded at me kindly and said, "Alright. Now for the left one."

I survived by reminding myself that delivering four children was far worse for my wife than what I was going through was for me. Even watching him "tie it off" (like watching a rodeo bull-roping over the horizon of my own belly) didn't faze me after that.

And of course, I was expected to come back in three weeks for the Test. I needed to wait for everything to heal, of course, and then contribute a sample to make sure there were no stray swimmers finding their way out into the world.

Now, I had read *The Water-Method Man* and had seen *Road Trip*; I had some preconceived notions (and not a little fear) of what this experience might involve. I was to be severely disappointed.

No hot nurse like the movies taught me to expect, and Dr. Pixie Face was nowhere to be found. Instead I got a middle-aged office drone with a greasy ponytail and weak, acne-scarred chin, handing me a cup and saying, "Fill this to here, hon, and get it back within 45 minutes."

I was shattered. Was there no special room for this, with porn or a fake boob or something? I didn't want to ask... I was still standing in the waiting room, and there were scads of people there! And the Baltimore beauty behind the desk had gone back to nibbling at a crab cake hidden behind her computer monitor. So I turned and left the office.

I left the building and returned furtively to my car where I stared at the cup. I knew from long experience that providing a sample wouldn't take much time, but where was I supposed to go? I only had (checking the clock) 40 minutes left, and home was twenty minutes away. Even if traffic was perfect, I only had a couple of minutes to try to produce a sample in a house full of screeching children! So I got out of the car and headed back into the building.

The bathrooms on the first three floors were either full of grunting patrons or cleaning crews. On the fifth floor, I finally found some isolation. It was a dingy, brown-tiled orifice of a room, with peeling paint on the stall doors and no provocative graffiti. And there, despite fearful internal warnings about George Michael's public indecency arrest intruding on what I was trying to visualize—I managed to produce my sample.

Handing the cup to the receptionist, I was confused when she looked surprised to see me. "That was quick, hon!" I thought she had said I had 45 minutes, though. "Oh, for the love! You have 45 minutes from when you fill the cup!" At that moment, it dawned on her, and a few of the bystanders, just what I had done, and where I had likely done it. So I left.

"Man," I thought to myself. "I'm never doing *that* again!"

11

When Does Magic Die?

"Oh, no... My tooth is still here!" said Mileidy.

My heart fell. My littlest had pulled her tooth out on a Saturday morning, and here it was on Sunday morning... and the Tooth Fairy has failed her.

She had been on something of a tooth-pulling spree lately. This was her third lost tooth in two weeks. I told her the Tooth Fairy probably hadn't expected her to lose another so quickly, and she seemed to accept that. "I'll just leave it for tonight," she said. "But I think I figured out who really brings the money."

Kate and I are not religious people, and we tried to be practical about child rearing; we didn't make up a lot of pretty lies about life. My children knew—as much as the innocent could know—what death was, who Jesus wasn't, and in general terms they knew how babies are made. They knew to call a vagina a "vagina" and a penis a "penis"—not a boom-boom or a wee-wee or a "private area," so in an emergency the doctor didn't have to guess where the injury was. They knew that there were Bad People out in the world, and that sometimes the Good People weren't at their best either.

We had a minor disagreement over whether to preserve some of the magic in our practical lives through observing the more obvious myths: the Tooth Fairy, Santa on Christmas Eve, and the Easter Bunny. Kate had fond memories of being surprised by gifts from the fantasy world, and she liked to make a big deal of keeping those occasions special. I had memories of being cautioned not to let those things distract me from Jesus. But neither of us had come into our own as sceptics at that point, and sentiment won out over our judgement.

I asked Mileidy who really brought the money with a quizzical expression, hoping I looked a bit like David Tennant's Dr. Who, and failing miserably, I'm sure.

"Your mom and dad," she said.

"You mean, *my* mom and dad?" I asked, hamming it up, hoping to talk my way out of this somehow. "But they're all the way out in Phoenix!"

"No," she explained in her exasperated way. "The mom and dad of the kid who lost the tooth." She probably wouldn't attain her dream of becoming a second-grade teacher with her short temper and her eye-rolling. "That means *you*, Dad."

"Well, I don't know anything about *that*," I said, unconvincingly. "You just put that tooth back under your pillow, and see what happens!" I asked to see it, and she proudly raised the pillow so I could. Hard to miss, tiny as it was; it was long, sharp, and still a little bloody, not unlike life itself.

I went along with her, partly out of cowardice, and partly because these fantasies *did* seem harmless enough…

Mileidy had a kind of filter on the world that bent the way she absorbed information. She had already reached the age where she noticed that her friends at school were talking about church and God, and she had even asked us about Easter.

We were driving around running errands, and the local churches had their "He is risen" signs up, which prompted her question. I did my best to explain the basics of the story; baby Jesus (from Christmas, remember?) grew up, and went around preaching. That made some people mad, so they killed him. Christians believe that three days after he was buried, he came back to life and walked around with his friends for 40 days before he rose up into the sky.

I thought that would do, as a rough overview.

A few days after telling her that, she was riding in the car again, and kept craning her neck to look out the window. Kate asked her what she was doing, and she said, "Daddy told me they killed baby Jesus and threw him up in the sky. I'm just trying to see if I can see him."

So, feeling guilty, I tucked her in, and kissed her, and went about my business. I had to wait for her to fall asleep, before I could do my Tooth Fairy duty. I tucked in the boys—Séamus, the elder, who had seen through our Tooth Fairy ruse years ago, and Lars, the younger, who knew damn well who was bringing the loot, and was still mad at us for being so stingy, but pretended to believe so the funds would keep flowing.

Bria and I went in the living room and fired up the TV so we could enjoy the adventures of the aforementioned Doctor, and I almost forgot about the tooth again. I only thought of it because of magic.

The particular episode we watched involved the Doctor and his companion visiting William Shakespeare in 1599, where they saved the universe by supplying the Bard of Avon with the word "Expelliarmus" at an opportune moment. The Harry Potter reference had us in stitches.

As I kissed Bria goodnight, she said something about how sad she had been on her 11th birthday, *not* finding out that she was a witch and going to Hogwarts. She's still a dreamer, today, and I am willing to bet she is watching out for a blue police box to appear on a street corner to whisk her away on an adventure... someday. Those dreams, no matter how silly or obviously false, those are part of us. They keep us going, for some reason.

I have my own dreams, my own private hopes, and if I told you what some of them were, you would think me a fool. You wouldn't believe that I could hold onto some of the things I dream about, as old as I am and as much as I have seen of the world. But I assure you, I do; and even though there is no reason to expect that they will, some of my dreams keep coming true.

I crept by one of my most precious dreams as she slumbered on my bed (waiting for her 0200 alarm—Kate had landed a job with the

Transportation Security Administration, and worked the early shift at the airport). I fetched one of the few remaining gold dollars I had hidden in my sock drawer for emergencies like this one—the coin had Andrew Jackson's face on it. Trying not to think about the irony of tucking the portrait of a mass murderer under my child's pillow, I crept up the stairs, in the dark, avoiding the creakier spots in the floor. And even though it was obviously false, and rather silly, I was the Tooth Fairy, and Old Hickory was the golden treasure.

When does the magic die? It didn't on that night.

Hopefully, it never will.

12
B.S. of America

My first ever Boy Scout meeting was not a success. Alright, technically it was Cub Scouts, since my sons would be a Tiger, and a Bear, respectively. The meeting was a first for all three of us. Except that it all seemed so very, very familiar somehow.

When I was in the third grade, my dad tried to get us involved in the Royal Ambassadors. That's the "Royal Ambassadors of Christ," by the way—the Southern Baptist Convention's version of Boy Scouts. We went to a few meetings at our church (which were like Sunday School, only on Wednesday nights), and one camping event. One. Some moron kept us up all night screaming along to "Father Abraham," and I was so exhausted that when I fell asleep, I wet my sleeping bag.

That tinge of Sunday School and psycho camp leaders, crossed with the psychological scarring left over from Air Force Basic Training—and I know I've blogged about *that* before—is what I'd been dreading since July, when Kate finally prevailed upon me to sign the boys up. She wore me down; convinced me that it wouldn't be like the R.A.s. That it wouldn't be like Girl Scouts, with the cookie sales and screaming girls. It was a lot more expensive than Girl Scouts, though, because the patches and awards came out of the dues. Fine. I would rather pay dues than do fund raisers.

Speaking of raising money, guess what we got to talk about first at our first ever meeting? That's right: we got the half hour sales lecture about how to sell popcorn. I guess cookies are too sissy.

It was the usual fundraising snow job you've seen if you have elementary school kids. They passed out the traditional glossy sheets with "fine, high-quality" prizes pictured next to perfectly reasonable goals. (Sell ten units, take home a talking light-up wristwatch!)

But, it was all for a good cause. After all, the money was used to fund our camping trip. Where we get to do fun things like the morning flag-raising, the evening vespers, and—if we're lucky—one of the priests will come along and have a mass on Saturday night!

Wait a holy minute there... what the fuck? I'm shilling popcorn so I can earn cheap trinkets and the chance to go out in the woods to worship fucking GOD with an alleged non-pedophile? My first meeting, and I already have to suffer through 30 minutes of live "paid TV," complete with screaming audience, not to mention a 15-minute sermon about earning a religion badge, and all so we can pay to go have church time in a forest?

Oh... oh, calm down... It's nonsectarian. They only require that you have "a" faith. They welcome all Christians, Jews, Muslims, Hindus, Ba'hai.... wait a minute. No Pastafarians? No room for di-agnostics? (FYI, that means I don't know if there's one god or two... but I can tell you what's wrong with *your* religion.)

I can hear the song and smell the urine as I write this.

Don't worry. I kept my mouth shut in the meeting. They didn't make me pray. They didn't make me swear fealty to any great mythical Beings. But they did slip in a few snide remarks about how "the Boy Scouts is one of the *few* organizations that still thinks getting closer to God is important." And somehow, that really wound me up. Are they completely clueless? Are they victims of Bill O'Reilly's fake "War on Christmas" conspiracy? Have they not heard about this George Bush guy that's moved into the White House? Honestly.

But the part that burned me up is that I felt like I had to do this. My boys and I needed something we could do together, and all three of us had demonstrated a deep disinterest in sports. The girls had Girl Scout time with Kate, and the boys did sound interested in camping and the pinewood racecars. I just wanted to give my boys something special, and make them feel like we were doing something together.

Kate felt terrible about the whole episode and did not insist on joining that group. She was as shocked by the tone of the meeting as I was, and she let them know when she called the pack leaders to make sure we had not paid them any money for dues, yet. They insisted that the meeting hadn't been at all like what I had described, so she asked if that bit about not "bearing false witness" was still in the Bible. And that would have been the end of that.

But, our Facebook friends offered a number of alternatives for us to try. We looked into Adventure Crew (our kids were too young still) and Camp Quest (not nearly local enough in those days); but in the end, there weren't a lot of workable options, and several people urged us to try a different pack.

This second pack also met in a church, but the leadership and other parents were a more diverse mix, and we even found some fellow sceptics already there. It still wasn't "my thing," and there would be moments of conflict over the years as the issue of allowing gay scouts and scout leaders to join the organization heated up; and there was the ever-present fact of our non-belief hanging between us and certain members of the troop and the council.

Still, there would be those moments that made it worthwhile for me, and there would even be times when the non-rustic, and decidedly non-handy Mr. Tad would find some welcome in a group of Scouts gathered around a campfire.

13
Roughing It Up

O, an Austrian went yodeling,
On a mountain so high,
When along came a *Cuckoo Bird*,
Interrupting his cry...

Winter Camp was the first of the major camping events which
were the main reason for joining the Cub Scouts. I'd been alternately
dreading and looking forward to it for months. Looking forward to the
parts that I know will be fun: hiking, games, good food, and playing
some guitar with folks. Dreading, because despite my cheerful
disposition, I'm still a cynic at heart, and I was pretty sure I knew what it
would be like: a dozen increasingly cranky adults surrounded by
increasingly smelly and insolent children. And do you know something?
I really hated being cynical, sometimes. So, I braced myself, held my
nose, and dived in. We're going to have fun, kids.

They were going to be out of school, they were bound to be sleep
deprived, and they would definitely outnumber us. Behold—I was about
to go camping with the zany and cacophonous *cuckoo birds*.

O, an Austrian went yodeling,
On a mountain so high,
When along came an *Avalanche*,
Interrupting his cry...

Trouble and woe seemed to pile on all at once, sometimes. Kate was coming down with something ominous; snow threatened to lay siege during the weekend; our car began flashing random warning lights—but only out the corner of my eye. I did *not* want to cancel this trip, but there were rumblings and creakings. Then we were off, and we made it, and dove into the tumult of the cabin.

Behold—the *avalanche!* —of boys, of sleeping bags, and piles of gear around the fireplace in a cabin in the woods.

O, an Austrian went yodeling,
On a mountain so high,
When along came a *Grizzly Bear*,
Interrupting his cry...

I was here to make sure—as Cubmaster Terry kept reminding us—that the Cub Scouts had fun, stayed safe, and learned something. I wasn't complaining about my lot; the group of adults in general was pretty good about keeping the kids out of trouble, making sure we were "two deep" (no adult was ever to be left alone with any number of children... even his own children), and making sure food-prep and cleanup happened. If anything, I felt like I wasn't completely pulling my weight. I kept showing up to the kitchen after everything was already cooked; I didn't quite make it back from escorting a group to the bathroom in time to clear the tables; I didn't know how to do most of the crafty stuff.

This left playground monitor as my fall-back duty—which, in its most common form, meant bellowing, "Quit that!" at the kids who insisted on pushing, shoving, and whacking each other with sticks. Behold—I was the *grizzly bear*. Grr, grr.

O, an Austrian went yodeling,
On a mountain so high,
When along came a *Saint Bernard*,

Interrupting his cry...

We were all fortunate to have a real, honest-to-goodness
professional medic along. By Saturday afternoon, the boys simply
couldn't hold back on their more violent tendencies, and two had to be
carried from the woods into the small cabin designated as the infirmary.
Nothing serious: a minor head wound and a twisted ankle. But they gave
Fred a chance to break out his kit and justify having dragged it up to
Northern Maryland for the weekend. Fortunately, these injuries were a
sufficient warning to the kids of the dangers of not listening to the
grizzly bears.

Behold—Fred was the *Saint Bernard,* bearing butterfly bandages,
an ice-pack, and an easy bedside manner—he had it all but the barrel of
whiskey around his neck (which was strictly forbidden on official
Scouting events).

O, an Austrian went yodeling,
On a mountain so high,
When along came a *Jersey Cow,*
Interrupting his cry...

One thing was not lacking in any way: the food. There was
plenty, and it was good. Mr. Harvey, with the assistance of his son,
Harvey Jr., has been the camp cook for 13 years. If what they say (that
you shouldn't trust a skinny cook) was true, then Mr. Harvey was one of
the most trustworthy cooks I'd ever run across. Everyone was full and
content, with nary a case of food poisoning in the bunch.

Behold—the Harveys were serving *cow,* roasting the beef and
mashing the potatoes.

O, an Austrian went yodeling,
On a mountain so high,
When along came a *Milking Maid,*
Interrupting his cry...

Among the scouts were a small group of siblings; mainly little sisters who were old enough to come along for the weekend. My own little princess came and immediately found a soulmate of the same age to spend the weekend with. But what to do when all of the adults are spread amongst the other camp activities? Enter the sweet 16-year-old daughter of the committee chairperson, young Dani. Dani was someone to watch over the little ones who were given their own cabin (no boys allowed), and to run interference (because a "No Boys Allowed" sign was like smearing honey around an ant hill) when the boys decided to storm the princesses' castle.

Behold—Dani was the *maid*, serving milk and cookies, and tending our wayward herd.

> O, an Austrian went yodeling,
> On a mountain so high,
> When along came the *Maid's Father*,
> Interrupting his cry...

I confess, I was not looking forward to a second night on the floor, with only a thin layer of foam between my bulk and the concrete and linoleum of the cabin. With the exception of the few moms and sisters, who took the counselor rooms in the back of the building, everyone slept in the big hall, heated by the massive wood stove at one end. The symphonic snoring of the first night hadn't bothered me, once the boys around us had settled down and stopped trying to keep each other awake. The noise was comical, but almost soothing, in a snorty, bandsaw-on-metal sort of way. Very rhythmic, and tidal. But my back was acting up after Friday's relatively brief night, and I wasn't looking forward to the certain agony facing me Sunday. All I could do was try to stay loose and tough it out. After all, I was committed to being the Entertainment at the Saturday night campfire.

Lars, the Tiger Cub, had woken on Saturday morning with a cough, and I tried to keep an eye on him throughout the day. I had to hold him in a chair by the fire and convince him to take a nap at one point, while Séamus and Mileidy ran about with their respective friends, doing whatever it is that healthy young people with energy do.

When he woke up, he asked to go home, so I told him that we could leave after dinner and the campfire ceremony. I may have been selfishly predisposed to make that change in our plans after dreading a second night on the cold floor in the Snore Tank. I didn't think Séamus or Mileidy would mind going home a little early. They had been showing signs of wearing down all afternoon, and I suspected that they missed their mom.

It worked out well enough. My back protested the extra exertions as I loaded the car, but I kept telling it, "Better to do it tonight than wait until morning!" It grudgingly agreed. I loaded the car between acts: dinner, load sleeping bags; cleanup, load suitcase; perform, load guitar. I felt guilty about bugging out the night before and leaving the bulk of the cleaning duties for the Sunday morning survivors, so I did some extra sweeping up and took a couple of bags of trash out to the dumpster.

By the time I was called up to perform, I was more than a little nervous. I wasn't sure the crowd would respond to my silly song; they saw the guitar, and started calling out requests. "Pantera!" "Play some Brad Paisley!" "Don't you know any good songs?" I ignored the 10-year-old heckler in the front row, though I imagined windmilling my guitar at him. But Harvey Jr. and Dani joined me as I started my main attraction.

"Ooooooooooohhhh.... an Austrian went yodeling..."

...and they loved it! They were entranced! They joined in with the noises and hand motions that went with each new character after each verse. I was a *hit*!

Alright, so that was all I had, but that was all I needed. They called for volunteers for jokes and stories, any other songs. We laughed, and sang, and it wasn't lame. What a relief.

Still, I needed to get the little ones home. There were some definite snuffles coming... maybe worse. But at least I went out with a...

Yodel-ee-yah, Kee-kee-yah,
Yodel-ee-yah cuckoo, cuckoo!
Swish,
Grrr,
Pant, pant
Squirt, squirt,
Smooch, smooch
BANG!

14
Going to Pet the Rabbits

Wednesday, May 25, 2011

I sat in a church this morning for the first time in many years.

The service was a memorial for the little daughter of a friend from work—a girl who had a degenerative condition called spinal muscular atrophy, which was expected to take her by age two. She made it almost to seven.

I have known a number of people who have carried the burden of watching a child fight for life against their own body. The cruelty of that burden is not in the caregiving of someone who is helpless and wholly dependent on you, but rather knowing that there is only one ending to this journey. There is no daring to hope, beyond the day-to-day needs and the occasional emergencies. These families have no choice but be strong and be prepared for the worst every minute... and they need to draw that strength from somewhere.

Being at a memorial service, we were there for the family's comfort. The songs they chose happened to be familiar to me, because I grew up with them; songs like "Amazing Grace" and "It Is Well With My Soul" were favorites with my childhood church.

I had forgotten until this morning how that latter song, by Horatio Spafford, is almost Zen in its imagery and message:

When peace like a river, attendeth my way,
When sorrows like sea billows roll;

Whatever my lot, Thou hast taught me to say,
It is well, it is well, with my soul.

Attaining peace in the tempest is a worthy goal. Calmness, at least, was something good and honest that could help my friend grieve. But then, as I sat listening to my friend's pastor talk about Heaven, I started to feel angry. My anger was not stirred up because he kept referring to God and Heaven as if they are real things—this was a church, after all. I can allow for poetic license and look for wisdom inside the stories.

The pastor began speaking, not just to his flock, but to all of us; and my anger sparked when he took the liberty of declaring that "we are all here to affirm what we know to be true: that there is a God and He is in control"—things that I don't know to be true, and do not affirm. This was a lie, and what's more, his body language and use of repetition and verbal sleight of hand showed me that he knew it was a lie.

I did not like being implicated in this lie, so I sat quietly out of respect for the grieving, but his repetition of that theme, and his flowery and precious descriptions of the things that the little girl would now be doing in Heaven—those empty words and fantasies stopped sounding like a comfort.

It reminded me of Steinbeck's *Of Mice and Men*—the pastor was George, spinning the fantastic story of a promised ranch full of puppies and bunnies, and I felt like Lenny. If you take a moment to review the plot summary (it ends badly for Lenny), I'm sure you'll understand when I say I felt creeped out.

Then, as a pastor is expected to do, he moved on from stealing his credibility from the presence of those gathered, to stealing the credit for the strength of my friend. I sat through his homily, fuming at the audacity of the trick and the lie at the core of it.

Raising *any* child is a challenge and a non-stop roller coaster of fear, risk, and heartbreak, interspersed with just enough joy to make it worthwhile. But for these parents, that joy can be bitter and elusive—and even a victory can be tragic. We cheapen these things in our culture with our perpetual tabloid stories and "disease of the week" movies—but families like these are quiet, epic heroes who are doing the impossible.

I don't blame any of them for leaning on something that I don't believe in. In the past I've made the mistake of referring to their faith as a crutch, but it really isn't that. A better analogy would be to compare it to weight-training or long-distance running; rather than a prop to support them, it is conditioning for facing reality in the long term instead of the short, escapist bursts the rest of us can get away with.

Most healthy and otherwise happy people I know can't face the prospect of a vast, cold, empty universe that doesn't care about them without falling to unreasoning pieces. How could I expect people under tremendous pressure to cope without giving that universe a name (God) and convincing themselves that despite all evidence to the contrary, it cares about them?

The stories we tell ourselves are how we remind ourselves what we are capable of doing. I have never balked when my friends needed to draw strength from these specific stories, and I don't think it would be helpful or kind to "correct" them when they tell me (and affirm to themselves) that their ability to persevere and overcome came from Jesus or God. If they were a baby flying elephant named Dumbo and told me the skill came from the Magic Feather they clutched in their trunk, I wouldn't distract them by arguing the physics of flight until they were safely on the ground.

But the truth is that wherever they think they're getting that strength, it's coming from within themselves—and being humans, that strength is an amazingly deep well. (Doctor Who says so all the time!)

My own break with faith came when I realized what a logical cheat the concept of God was. Those speaking on God's behalf love to tell us that everything good comes from God, and is solely to God's credit. Without God, we are not capable of anything at all. And what about all of our failures and sins? That's all on us. Me, specifically. Or you.

As I grew up, and realized that I was expected to surrender to this double whammy of self-denial, I balked. I assumed at first that was just my sinful pride talking. Saying to oneself that it isn't fair that I have to do all the work and give God the glory sounds exactly like what Satan is supposed to have said, but considering who taught me the Satan story, the ruse became transparent. I came to understand that this God seemed not to take care of my homework or my auto maintenance or my bills without a heck of a lot of assistance from me, and if I was taking care of myself, I didn't need to run myself down with a story that made me the bad guy.

All of that nonsense is a logical trap designed to prey on those who need to tell themselves that there is a source of strength outside themselves that they can't live without. To defy the pastor is to put the source of their strength at risk; to question his logic is to risk their faith in themselves. So the pastor tells them their own strength is an unreliable and dangerous flaw, and that they should trust in God—and that someday, we'll have a ranch where we can pet the rabbits. Just like Lenny.

I don't mean to trivialize this. I watch people suffer through awful things in life all the time. They call on their God, and sometimes, when they stop crying and dig down deep, they find something inside themselves that gets them through. Sometimes it's just a matter of letting go—of becoming the water, if you will—and they can cope. They pull themselves through. Then they thank God for it.

So I sat in a church this morning for the first time in many years, listening to my friend's pastor talk about God, and about her strength, and I realized that I, as a non-believer, could see something in her that no believer really sees. They pay lip service to her, but then steal her credit and attribute it to God—a construct meant to put a happy face on a cold, brutal universe.

And while they do that to her, I realize that as a non-believer, I can see what is really divine.

17
Asians In My Way

I like to think I've outgrown a lot of bad habits. Poor reasoning, sloppy thinking, lazy shortcuts—I work on getting rid of these. But I'm like most of you; I'm not perfect, and humor is my weakness.

You have to be careful with humor. Even if you think you're just kidding you have to be careful that you're not hurting someone with it. Like the earlier stories of my life in Korean school, I don't tell these stories to disparage other people. I tell them to illustrate the difference between anecdotes and stereotypes, to show the dangers of confirmation bias, and to make fun of myself.

I have long suffered from the persistent notion that Asian people are conspiring to get in my way. Rationally, I know that this is not so, and I look for ways to subvert my brain's tendency to reinforce that notion, but as you will see, I have not been entirely successful. So, when you read this and think, "Christ, you're an asshole"—that's kinda my point. As the *Avenue Q* song goes, "Everyone's a little bit racist." I might as well use my own racism as a cautionary tale.

My first confrontation with this Asians In My Way phenomenon began (not on Avenue Q) on the Pacific Coast Highway in 1995. My lovely bride and I were just beginning our whirlwind romance, and we pulled off the road on a cliff-side where there was a convenience store and a magnificent view of the ocean. We returned to Kate's sporty little Saturn intending to head further south, but found that we were blocked in by a tour bus full of Asian tourists. There were several dozen of them standing as a group behind our car, with their bus (and the remarkable view) behind them. The driver was trying to take a picture of the group with each of their cameras. He must have had 30 cameras hanging on his arms, and he was working his way through all of them.

Just when we thought he was done, a few more cameras would be produced, and he would keep going—this happened more than once. We waited. We waited some more. Finally, Kate had a brilliant idea. She handed her own camera to the tour guide, and we stood next to the group and got our own photo out of the deal.

The group seemed confused... but did not take the hint.

Eventually they did disperse to go buy snacks, and we made our escape, laughing at the bemused expressions they gave us as we fled.

That might have been the end of it, but for two related events. First, I saw a comedian on TV joking about the stereotypical Asian tourists who experience the world only through their cameras. Second, we went to the zoo.

A small group of us visited Marine World/Africa USA in Valencia, California, one glorious spring weekend. The Africa exhibits were newly opened, and they promised a more realistic experience than traditional zoos. As it happened, the natural designs of the enclosures coincided with the time of year to provide us with a glimpse of the romantic life of the animals. We passed several exhibits in which amorous couples coupled, hurrying past to avoid seeming perversely intrusive, and giggling at the comments we overheard from other patrons. ("Mommy, why is that zebra pushing the other zebra around the pen?")

We arrived at the rhinoceros enclosure behind a crowd of tourists (yes, they were Asian) who were gathered around a park ranger. The tourists bristled with the latest video recording technologies and pressed against the railing, making it impossible for us to see what the excitement was about. When we finally squeezed into a gap, we saw the two rhinos at opposite ends of the pen. The female was contentedly sunning herself in the dust while the male stood sullenly in a corner with his back to the crowd of humans.

While we watched, we noticed that his penis was extended, bending toward the earth like a third hind leg, and the rhino was tapping the tip on the ground the way a nervous person might drum his finger on a table while waiting for service in a restaurant. Every few seconds, he would take a huge, shuddering breath and sigh deeply before resuming his tapping.

Angie interrupted the ranger, who was trying to explain the daily dietary regimen to an uninterested crowd, and asked, "Why is he doing... that?"

The ranger sighed and said, "It is mating season. But rhinoceroses mate in herds, and we only have two. Since he doesn't have a whole group of cows, he feels like he can't catch this female. So he's... frustrated."

As she delivered that last word, the male rhino took a step forward and stepped on the tip of his dusty member with his huge, horny foot. An excited murmur rose from the crowd as they adjusted cameras and presumably translated what the ranger had said for the audience back home. The rhino leaned from side to side, trying to tug his penis loose from his own weight, and as he did so, the rhino ripped the most amazing fart any of us had ever experienced. It vibrated out of him with an unmistakable noise, sustained for an impossible length of time. The crowd went silent in awe at the gastrointestinal virtuosity of the great beast.

When the rhino stopped, the ranger calmly broke the shocked silence: "They have a high fiber diet," she shrugged. The tourists responded only by angling for a better angle to record this magnificence.

Clearly, these episodes cemented that camera-wielding, crowding, clustering stereotype in my mind. I tried not to think of Asian people that way, but I was still attending the Korean language school, and a day didn't pass without someone from Korea colliding with me in the hallway or nearly clipping me as they drove by—even when no cameras were involved. I had to struggle to convince myself that they weren't aiming for me, especially in the broad hallways of the school, where despite having plenty of room for four people to pass each other abreast I would find myself crowded against the wall by one of my teachers. Even when I flunked out of Korean school and started taking Russian, I noticed that everywhere I went, there were Asians in my way!

I commented on this to a few of my friends, and most of them laughed at me ("Christ, you're an asshole!") but those closest to me noticed it, too. I'd be at the grocery store, and an oblivious Chinese woman would block me at every aisle with her shopping cart. I'd try to exit the freeway, get cut off by someone in a minivan and forced to take the next exit, only to see an Asian face glaring back at me. It became a running joke—one that I tended to keep to myself, because, after all, I didn't want to seem racist.

The root of my problem is that the human brain has evolved to spot patterns in our surroundings, and once you think you've noticed a pattern, you start looking for that pattern whether you realize it or not. We also evolved to sort and categorize things, including people. Now that my brain has equated this category of people ("Asians") with this pattern ("you're in my way"), it tries to convince me that this is inevitable no matter where I go.

Eventually, we left California and ended up in Maryland. One of our favorite things to do was to take our wee bairn out and push her around Washington, DC, in her stroller. On one particularly sunny day, we headed for the Smithsonian Natural History Museum to see if Bria would enjoy looking at dinosaurs. (She did!)

The museum was pretty crowded, but there was one family that seemed to dog our steps around every corner. We ran into them several times, and tried to slow down so they'd get ahead of us. They slowed down, too. We pushed through the clot of them and sped up to get away from them, and they kept pace, pushing us from behind. It was maddening. But we figured we'd lose track of them when the baby needed to be fed and changed, and we set up camp in the family restroom.

When we were done, a good 15 minutes had passed, and I went out to retrieve our stroller—only to walk straight into the lens of our shadow family's video camera.

Because I had heard them speaking Korean (I sucked at it, but I could identify it like a champ), I tried saying excuse me—"shi-leh hamnida"—but that didn't work. No one made eye contact (they seemed to think that would be rude) and they just bunched up around the cameraman, becoming intensely interested in the woolly mammoth he was filming. I tried to maneuver behind them, to avoid being rude myself by walking in front of the camera—but they were kind of milling around and there always seemed to be an elbow or knee wherever I was trying to slide by, and no amount of *shi-leh hamnida* got me anywhere.

My Korean teachers had impressed upon us the importance that manners have in their culture. Being mostly uncouth youths fresh out of the Midwest, we pestered them to teach us bad words and they always demurred, claiming that the worst thing you could say to any Korean would be to address them with the wrong verb construction, indicating that you thought you had a higher status than the person you were speaking to. That hadn't stopped us from looking up words that (we hoped) would express some of the important phrases that we frequently used on each other.

So, I decided to be rude, and finally pushed my way in front of Mr. Cameraman. Naturally, he pressed forward so I found myself mouth-to-microphone with his camera, and I said what the rude, angry American inside me had wanted to say all along: "Jaji mog-ko," which was my best attempt at, "Eat a dick."

Now, as poor as my language skill was (and is), it was possible that this would mean nothing to him or his audience, but I imagine that they took that tape home to Korea with them, and invited all of their neighbors and relatives to a big "Trip to America" movie night. I like to imagine them all gathered in front of the largest TV that Samsung made in 1997, with their most ancient, honored grandmother seated right up front. I am sure Mr. Cameraman said, "Honored grandmother, behold the woolly mammoth I filmed for you at the Natural History Museum" ...just as the mammoth on screen rumbled, "Eat a dick," in a good ol' U.S. accent.

It is possible that I may have killed an old Korean grandmother in 1997, and I would never know.

Naturally, I don't keep these little stories to myself, and I have told them many times to my best of friends. A couple of years ago, my friend Brent, from my Russian class, reconnected on Facebook with a German woman he had befriended while he was stationed in Germany ten years before. She came to America for a visit, and I drove him to the airport in Philadelphia to meet her. On the way back to Baltimore, I got drawn into telling her these stories. We had a few laughs, and I explained that I don't really harbor any lasting resentment, but that I always seem to find Asians in my way—and I cautioned her to watch out if she visited DC.

As it happened, Brent took her to see the Capital Mall, and while they were reading one of the quotes set into the paving stones of the World War II Memorial, an odd thing happened.

They were standing in a relatively open space, obviously reading a plaque on the ground, and an elderly Asian man walked up to them and stood in front of them, placing his feet on the square they were reading. They looked up at him, and he began shaking some kind of wooden clacking device—CLACK-A-CLACK-A-CLACK-A—as he stared right back at them.

CLACK-A-CLACK-A-CLACK-A

"Excuse us, sir..."

CLACK-A-CLACK-A-CLACK-A

"We were reading that!"

A crowd gathered—most likely a tour group, since they were, as you've guessed, Asian—pressing the two would-be readers off to the side. Everyone in the group kept staring at them, as if they were the ones in the way, and while no one intentionally shoved them, they were nudged further and further away until they decided to give up and head for less crowded territory.

Naturally, they thought of me. The experience was odd, but the fact that an Asian tour group was involved after my stories made me seem prophetic. When my German friend told me about this adventure, I had to laugh. "It looks like I passed my curse on to you!" I told her. "Confirmation bias—it's a terrible, terrible thing!" We all laughed then, and thought nothing more about it... until she landed in Munich on her return trip home, and Asians started showing up everywhere. Blocking her way off the train, nudging her away from the baggage claim...

Of course, now that I've told you all of this, you're bound to start noticing it, too. There are one billion people in China alone, which means you've got a better than one-in-seven chance that anyone you meet on this planet would fit the definition of "Asian," and now every time you see one of them, you're going to register the experience in the back of your head. Even though you're probably cut off in traffic a hundred times a day, you'll only notice the Asians. Even though you're more likely to get bumped in the grocery store by old white people, you'll notice the Asians.

Just remember that it isn't their fault—it's my fault, and my curse. And even though I know it's my brain following its own confirmation bias, I will continue to find #AsiansInMyWay. And to them I can only (and will only) say, "Excuse me."

"실례합니다."

"对不起. "

"ちょっと失礼します。."

"ขอโทษ."

"Xin lôi."

18

Reunions

The committees for the Cactus High School classes of 1989 and 1990 decided to pool their resources and organize a twenty-year reunion together, so the Class Reunion of 1989/1990 was held in Glendale, Arizona, in February 2010.

I was pretty surprised that Michelle was willing to drive all the way out to my parents' house to practice our songs for the reunion. Even in high school—that can't have been 20 years ago already, can it?—we lived pretty far off the beaten path, but after I left for the Air Force, Mom and Dad bought property even further out, moving nearly to Wickenburg. That added a good 25 miles to their already lengthy commutes.

But Michelle said she was used to driving all over the Valley of the Sun for her job, and didn't mind. So there we were, playing music and talking about old times and recent times, and about our apprehensions of the reunion itself. Would we remember the people who showed up? Would they remember us? Fondly? Would our best friends be there, or would they be stuck in far-flung corners of the world?

We needn't have worried.

Even 10 years ago, documenting this would have been more difficult; putting memories down in a blog or sharing pictures on Facebook was either unheard of, or at least uncommon. But now, roaming through a hotel ballroom full of not-so-distant strangers is a matter of recognition more than anything: how much do they resemble their profile pictures? And can you read their name tag in the dim light? Most of the ice-breaking has already happened online.

So, for me at least, the evening was a stream of people who looked a lot like the parents of the kids I knew in high school, walking around, being happy to see each other. Michelle and I each circulated for a while before heading up to the makeshift stage.

The DJ had a small stack of speakers, and three rarely-used microphones. Our classmates seemed to enjoy our singing, even though the PA system we had wasn't quite up to the task of filling the room. They may not have been able to hear the songs well enough to tell them apart, but they seemed to appreciate our effort. We gave them an acoustic rendition of "Sweet Child O'Mine," which was a radio hit that no one had been able to escape in 1989, and we did "Leaving On a Jet Plane," which had been one of the songs our band and choir groups had often sung together on the bus trips across Arizona to compete in All-State competitions.

Afterward, we found our old gang. Most of them were alive and (relatively) healthy. There were a few missing who are no longer with us, and a few I never would have expected to make it this far (and I'm glad you did!).

In a lot of ways, we hadn't changed. The patterns of who talked to whom, who got silly-drunk and who withdrew early, the inevitable comparisons of work, hobbies, family, successes and failures; that all stayed the same.

I wished for the thousandth time that I could have brought Kate to this event with me, but we couldn't afford the extra plane ticket. She would have been pretty uncomfortable, anyway, trying to make small talk with complete strangers. And a trip like that would only serve to remind her that we haven't been able to find a way to move back to the land of sunshine and open sky that she fell in love with the first time I brought her home.

Throughout the evening, I tried not to dwell on my failures. Most of the people I ran into were happy to see me; some of them had read my blog and they saw the pictures I posted of the kids, so I didn't have to explain much about what I'd been up to—though there was a vaguely risqué running joke about my wife being imaginary that kept drawing laughs throughout the night. (After all, what would a gorgeous person like her want with a dork like me after twenty years?) They didn't mean anything by the joke, but I had to keep reminding myself of that fact. They couldn't know the darker details behind my funny stories, or how close my family had come to real disaster.

They could probably guess how bad things had been, if they thought about it that deeply. We have four kids and have moved across continents and oceans on a shoestring budget, after all; but they couldn't really know what our misadventures did to my marriage, or what it took for Kate and me to come out on the other side, still together. I could tell from the way some of their own stories trailed off into awkward pauses how much they'd really been through themselves, but time or shyness made them stick to just the highlights about their lives.

Still, as the awkwardness wore off and the night wore on, the crowd began to thin, and those of us who stayed compared more stories and relaxed. I probably told them a few of the tales you just read. They told me a few of their own, and shared gossip about those who hadn't attended the reunion. We left a lot unsaid, hoping that there would be another night like this when we could say more.

As we looked around at each other, nodding in approval, I saw a truth unfold at my 20-year high school reunion that I barely dared hope would be true all those years ago.

We kids really are "okay."

About the Author

Tad Callin has been a lot of things, but he is most proud of being a father of four, a husband of one, and writer of much. In addition to *Tad's Happy Funtime*, Tad is the author of an urban fantasy story called "Silver," published by the *The Dunesteef Audio Fiction Magazine*, and a genealogical book of Callin family history called, of course, *The Callin Family History*. His science fiction novel tentatively entitled *Airborne* (you learned it here first) is due in 2017.

Originally from the Southwest, Tad hopes to return there with his family, but until then he'll keep exploring his adopted hometown of Baltimore.

Proof

Made in the USA
Charleston, SC
30 March 2016